THE MEMOIR PROJECT

THE MEMOIR PROJECT

A THOROUGHLY NON-STANDARDIZED
TEXT FOR WRITING & LIFE

MARION ROACH SMITH

GRAND CENTRAL
PUBLISHING

NEW YORK   BOSTON

Grand Central Publishing
Hachette Book Group
1290 Avenue of the Americas
New York, NY 10104

www.HachetteBookGroup.com

Printed in the United States of America

First Edition: June 2011

10 9 8 7

Grand Central Publishing is a division of Hachette Book Group, Inc. The Grand Central Publishing name and logo is a trademark of Hachette Book Group, Inc.

Library of Congress Cataloging-in-Publication Data
Roach Smith, Marion
    The memoir project : a thoroughly non-standardized text for writing &
life / Marion Roach Smith.— 1st ed.
        p. cm.
    ISBN 978-0-446-58484-5
    1. Autobiography—Authorship—Handbooks, manuals, etc.   I. Title.
CT25.R62 2011
808'.06692—dc22
                                                                    2010041019

For Richard Young

Contents

There is an old saying
that most men would rather
have you hear their story
than grant their wish.

Required Reading

THIS IS A SIMPLE tale. I was born in the Little Neck Public Library in Queens, New York. Next to the card catalogue. Well, that's the way I remember it, and I'm sticking to that story, no matter what. Go into therapy and you are likely to be asked, "What is your first memory?" And for many people, this is a rare opportunity to unlock the floodgates, remove the tourniquet, and let the platelets flow. But when I want to investigate myself, I type, and when I ask myself to re-create those first moments, what gets typed up is me standing on my tiptoes, peering into a card catalogue.

It was a long wooden drawer that may have pulled out for a mile and a half. Like a great straight snake, right at hip bone level to my mother, exactly at eye level to me, it slid out and I waited.

"I want you to see something," I think she said.

A gorgeous woman; I would have done anything she told me. This was the person who held the keys to the kingdom of power, the parent who had taught me to read, sitting with me as one day the letters turned into words, and the words into sentences, and the sentences into the authority that every child craves—to learn, to retell, and to entertain. My mother's red fingernails, lacquered to match her lips, were flipping like sexy windshield wipers through the cards, one after the other. Where were we going this time? I wondered. Maybe I was five. We had long before run through the Golden Books and had recently been to meet *Black Beauty*, and we were about to read

The Pushcart War, a book about the Lower East Side. We had dabbled in poetry and had read of the requisite heroes and demons of the Bible.

Suddenly, she stopped, lifting up a single card. On it was my father's name: James P. Roach.

"Look at that!" she said. "Isn't that wonderful?"

It was. In that snug, long drawer, there for the world to stumble upon, to cross-reference, to *read*: my dad. A sportswriter, he was in the card catalogue. Other girls wanted to be veterinarians, to marry rich, to be Rockettes. From that moment on, what I wanted most was a place of my own in the Dewey decimal system.

Shortly after that day, we moved into a house with a den in which was placed a desk and a typewriter, and that's where I watched my father write on deadline. It was there that he was discovered one afternoon, sitting hunched over that typewriter, running his hands through his thin hair. For the previous three days, painters had been in the house changing the color of every single room to champagne—the white of the 1970s. On the fourth day of this monotonous work, a lone painter followed the sound of the clacking keys. The encounter went something like this:

"Mr. Roach," said the painter.

Mr. Roach looked up and said nothing.

"It seems a shame," the painter continued.

Mr. Roach said, "Who are you?"

"The painter?" the man asked, now unsure himself.

"Yes." My father looked back to his blank page.

"That dining room. You want that champagne, too?"

"Champagne?"

"Like the rest of the rooms?"

"The *rest* of the rooms?"

"Are champagne."

"In *this* house? Since when?"

"Thursday."

"And the dining room?"

"Not yet."

The writer cast a look at the clock, the typewriter, then the painter. The story was due. "What nationality are you?" he asked.

"Huh?"

"Nationality."

"Croatian," said the painter.

"Such lovely national colors," said the writer. "Use those."

Back to the typewriter, the assignment, and the silence—which was broken six hours later by the earsplitting scream of a woman viewing her red, white, and brown dining room for the first time. It may have been the only time Jim Roach expressed himself in anything other than words in his own home. But it is worth noting that the dining room walls remained a deep red, the ceiling a pure white, and the beams their natural brown for as long as we had the house.

It seemed to me that to get into the stacks of the library, writers had to keep their heads down, no matter the consequences.

And writing does have consequences. Especially if you tell the truth, which is what memoir requires. When my friend Elizabeth recently found out that she has multiple sclerosis (MS), she thought about that for a while and then wrote an op-ed piece for the *Los Angeles Times*. Some years before, via in vitro fertilization, she had gotten pregnant, given birth, and then donated some of her unused embryos to science. After her MS diagnosis, she wrote how she wished those cells had gone toward fetal tissue research for her illness and others. Upon publication, accolades came in from her peers, but she also had to ditch her home phone number because of the phalanx of wingnuts calling to say they would have adopted those embryos.

On some level you've always known that consequences lurk when telling your tale—a chill from the family, crank calls on your telephone, or perhaps a unique terror that comes from retracing something to its beginning to understand the power it has over your life. Which is why this morning, when you could have been writing, you rechecked your closet for what you'll wear on the *Today* show during your book tour.

Today may or may not be in your future, but what is entirely possible is that you'll lose somebody's affections if you tell the truth. However, I am quite sure that if you tell the truth, you will feel something real. "Feeling something real" is where I prefer to live, trying to palpate the small moments of life, the moments of intuition, the places where we fail and where we change. Right now my life is packed with middle-aged friends engaged in all manner of dangerous behaviors again—the ones they forgot we did in our twenties. They insist that they are merely trying to *feel something*. I suggest honestly writing about your life. You'll feel something. I promise.

But first, you have to agree to be taught. This is harder than it sounds. Which is why I start the book off not with a classic introduction but with an opener called "Required Reading." Because like everyone who wants to write a memoir—via writing vignettes expressly for their children to read, blogging, writing essays, or taking on an entire book—you want to skip the intro and get right to the part where I assign you the writing exercises, prompts, or bulleted list of killer tips that will fritter away the time until you buy your next book on writing.

You won't find any of those insulting tasks here. From this moment on, you are writing with purpose and are no longer merely practicing. You are writing with intent. So read the book and follow the advice.

And write.

———

There once was a time when I was terribly polite about this work and what it requires. At cocktail parties, when someone asked me what I do, I'd smile just above my string of pearls and reply, "I'm a writer," and nearly to a person, he'd say he was going to write when he retired. Nodding, I'd wish him the best with it and slink off to find the canapés, wondering what was wrong with me that I was going to devote my whole life to writing, when clearly people who were smarter than I could put it off until they got around to it.

Now I'm not so polite. Now, when someone tells me that he is going to become a writer when he gets around to it, I reply, "And what do you do?" And sometimes he says, "Oh, I'm a brain surgeon," and that's my favorite reply. Then I can say, "When I retire, I'm going to become a brain surgeon," with just a hint of a sneer above those pearls.

This is serious work. And it cannot be reduced to generic writing exercises and prefabricated prompts. And ask yourself these questions: Have any of those ditties ever gotten you published? Has scribbling from the right side of your brain, or getting in touch with your angel's feather, or keeping morning pages put you where you want to be as a writer? After reading one of those books of exercises, or subscribing to yet another Web-based, prompt-list newsletter, have you actually finished that letter to your child that you long to give her? I doubt it. I suspect that those manners of nonsense have instead stolen what little time you had for writing.

How do I know? Because my classes are filled with people *recovering* from those very exercises, people whose sole relationship to writing was practicing. Also in my classes: aspiring authors who detoured into inertia after listening to parents, spouses, nuns, or teachers tell them that memoir writing has no value.

Its value is inestimable. Which is why you have to be taught to do it.

Right out of college, I got a job at the *New York Times*, where I met a fine editor who was roundly disliked by his peers. I always suspected he was unpopular because he had a slogan under the Plexiglas top of his desk that read, "I believe in learning the craft of writing." He would actually sit with young writers and help craft their stories, and in doing so, craft the writers themselves. Pretty much everyone else there assumed that you came fully loaded to the *Times*. I did not. I wasn't very good, but I was better when I left. Most of the other people at the *Times* would just as soon have ripped a hunk out of your thigh as help you, but not this guy. And so, of course, he became known as being soft and was soon moved someplace where he'd do less damage than he apparently did by encouraging young people to write.

You have to agree to be taught because there is no reason in the world that you should know how to do this. Which aspect of your life could possibly prepare you to sit alone in a room, day after day, with your own thoughts, reach down, pull up only those ideas that apply to the topic at hand, toss the others aside, and marshal the ones needed into logical, entertaining order on deadline? That's why most people just talk about the books they are going to write, and few actually write them. Journalists who do this are referred to by their peers as "talking journalists," and not with any affection, especially when they monopolize dinner parties with rollicking tales from the book they keep meaning to write. Unwittingly, they are revealing just how hard this is. Alone in a room with their own thoughts, they focus on how the color of the trim clashes with the color of the walls, or how very much they want to cultivate exotic orchids. Who could write under those conditions?

It's like that old joke: An elderly guy hires a hooker, goes to a motel, and lies down on the bed, telling her that before he can perform, she must go into the bathroom and run the shower so that it sounds as if it's raining. She does, and then comes back to the bedroom only to be sent back into the bathroom to shake the shower curtain and make the sound of thunder. She does, and getting just the tiniest bit exasperated, she returns to see him sprawled on the bed. "Turn the light on and off," he says. "Make like it's lightning." So she's banging the shower curtain, the water is pounding onto the porcelain tub, and she's turning the light on and off, calling to him from the bathroom, "Are we going to do this? You know, have sex?" And the old man shrugs, calling back, "What, in this weather?"

To write, you have to ignore the weather, which is made up of every manner of distraction you know, including those books of writing exercises.

You want to write? Then let's write. Maybe it is only now occurring to you that you want to write down some scenes from your life. That's wonderful, since it is never too late—or too early—to begin. Perhaps this book was a gift from someone who wants to read those tales you tell. What a lovely compliment the giver is offering by encouraging you to write it all down. Don't worry if you think of yourself as inexperienced: You'll be fine. One of the few things I know for certain is that everyone has a story. Also, whether you are a beginner or someone who has written for years, your challenges are nearly the same, since memoir writing is a great equalizer, smoothing the playing field to a large degree, while pocking it with the very same hazards for all.

And don't worry if you've never kept a journal, notebook, or scrapbook and can't imagine how you'll remember the details of life. Throughout this book I am going to tell you tales that will stir up your subconscious, as well as teach you methods for researching your own life. We'll get to your material. I promise.

So let's begin together, literally on the same page, and with a tacit agreement that from this moment on, we will write no exercises; we will write for real. With a goal. Maybe that goal is to get on NPR. Good. The back page of the *New York Times Magazine*, perhaps? Fine. Maybe you want to publish a book? Great. Maybe your intent is to give your spouse the gift of a tale from your marriage. Perfect. Maybe it's to tell your kids the story of their ancestors' emigration, or about the crazy middle-of-the-night rush to the hospital that resulted in their births. Even better. And here's some good news: When you write memoir, you'll be writing what you know. That's right: what you already know. From now on, that's your job, and nowhere in that job description does it include lighting a scented candle, throwing on a shawl, and scribbling exercises or prompts in a notebook until you get bored and head back to your macramé.

From this minute forward, your intent is to write with purpose. And trust me when I tell you that the difference between morning pages and writing with purpose is the difference between a wish and a prayer.

Not long after my father's encounter with the painter, a family vacation in the Caribbean brought into my life what I now call "cheeky birds." A creative taxonomist, my father cavorted with language, hybridizing terms that cross-bred his British heritage with American expressions. When we were small, and still under the spell of believing everything he said to be true, I'd point to a dog, for instance, and ask my dad its breed. He'd nod sagely and reply, "North American Under-Brogan." It was some years before I understood that miniscule mutts who got underfoot were not, in fact, named for an obscure English word for "shoe."

I've come to think of memoirists as the cheeky birds of writers, "cheek" being a British word for "bold." The brash creatures to whom my dad bestowed this name distinguished themselves by swooping onto our hotel patio to perch on our plates, balance on our pencils, and eat from our hands. This is what you are now allowed to do—to glide into the banquet that is your tale and take what you need from the feast. By the time you finish this book, you will have a new appreciation of your very own bird's-eye view and what it is you can do with it when you write.

And when you do, things will change, since the transition to reporting on one's own life can reap breathtaking results. After you learn how to truly observe the life you live, the result may be excellence—in both the writing and in the living. And when my students look unconvinced and start to shift in their seats, I tell them the story of Arthur Miller and his uncle Manny Newman, the salesman who committed suicide and whose two sons Miller interviewed before writing his great play *Death of a Salesman*. And then I tell them about the brave woman in my class who presented her dying husband the book-length story of their wonderful union on their fiftieth wedding anniversary. And then I tell them about my first autopsy.

A few years ago, while writing a book, I went behind the scenes in the world of forensic science, attending forensic entomology school and blood-spatter-analysis class, and somehow I managed not only to enter the morgue but also to stay for a five-and-a-half-hour autopsy, my first.

And it was there, as the fear subsided, that I inched closer to the body of a man dead ten days, and marveled at the connection between things. In the big experience, it was the small things that changed me: The rib cage's perfect arch harboring the heart made me weep; witnessing it felt like a near occasion to faith.

The morgue also presented some unique metaphors for understanding writing, the most profound of which was there in the spine: the vertebrae, those odd individual muffins of bone that hold us together. Take one out, weigh it in your hand, bounce it up and down and have a look at it, and that's an essay, or a blog post, each of which must be as precisely designed as individual vertebrae. Snap that vertebra back into being an essential part of the spine and the spine is whole again, much like a long-form memoir.

Seeing our connections, considering them, describing them—that's where writing what you know begins. I'm quite sure of that, as well as of a few more things, at least when it comes to writing memoir.

Here they are.

Chapter 1

You Must Be Present to Win

FLANNERY O'CONNOR SAID that anyone who survives childhood has enough material to write for the rest of her life. She's right. Writing about yourself and your crazy (or not-so-crazy) family can be the big vein, if you're ready. But if you're not, it's the brick wall. Indeed, the single biggest reason for not being prepared to write what you know is not knowing how to dig among your stuff to get what you need.

So let's see if we can correct that.

In any decent game of chance, you must be present to win. That's also true with writing what you know, where paying attention is the skill you need to succeed. What you pay attention to is detail, and that skill is like sorting jewelry: Get a good loupe, learn to focus it, and then scramble amid your dazzling, jagged facets for only those few pieces that need apply.

What Ernest Hemingway taught us in the last century still gives good weight: What you leave out of the story is perhaps more important than what you put in. It does me no good to know someone's height, weight, and eye color, if those details do not drive your story forward. No matter what the level of general writing experience students have, when new to memoir, writers tend to relate when they were born, what someone else looks like, or the exact years during which they attended elementary school. Writing memoir does require including accurate facts, but writing good memoir requires more than that, and it begins with paying a particular sort of attention.

William Maxwell, the fiction editor of the *New Yorker* for more than forty years—he edited John Updike and John O'Hara and John Cheever—was a marvelous fiction and nonfiction writer in his own right. He believed that to write, all you need is to remember the slam of your childhood home's screen door. He's right, too, because you have what you need to write what you know. Just like Dorothy's ruby-red shoes, you've had it on you all the time. It's what you've been doing with those details that's the problem, if you've either done nothing, have been wasting precious time on mere exercises, or are under the mistaken belief that anyone might eagerly slog through pages of facts about your life.

To transpose your life's details into real content—to write with intent—I'd add to the Flannery-Ernest-William adages that you must be hospitable. I have only one maxim in my office, on a little index card. It reads, "Be hospitable." And it has been there through four books, countless magazine pieces, radio essays, blog posts, and op-eds.

I've read that the great screenwriter Paddy Chayefsky kept a little nudge on his desk that said, "He gets it," and I understand how that could be the sole encouragement a screenwriter might need. In any good movie, someone has to change and be transformed. He will reach some transcendence, no matter how small. To do so, the protagonist must "get" the idea in play. For you to get the idea of writing memoir with intent, I suggest you be hospitable, though it's harder than it sounds.

THE WAY YOU WEAR YOUR HAT, THE WAY YOU SIP YOUR TEA

Being hospitable begins with preparing a clean, well-lighted desk, and reporting to it each day, at the same time if possible. Even if forty-five minutes is all you can allot, allot it and show up. Woody Allen said that 80 percent of success is showing up, and while he's right, I'd remind you that showing up at a desk with overdue income-tax forms on it doesn't work. Almost to a person, my students who are in recovery from mere writing exercises report that they write in bed or while cadging a moment at the bus stop or kitchen table, tucking in writing as time allows.

I suggest you try a little hospitality instead. Being hospitable requires that you slow down the process and do some reporting before you begin to write. Carry an index card in a pocket and in your wallet, and the next time you watch Meryl Streep transport herself from one emotion to the next, note the spare gesture she employs. Capture effective dialogue you overhear. When you attend your daughter's fourth-grade piano recital, jot down an impression or two. It's okay, I promise, since it beats the hell out of all those other parents texting on their BlackBerries. I keep several running lists in a notebook in my car, from titles of those songs that are the soundtrack of my life, to those new and different things people seem to need to do while driving. At some point, I'll turn them into pieces, but I can't use these details later if I don't have them. And don't expect to carry these home in your head. Instead, write them down. And while I do shun those people texting at their children's performances, in other spaces, personal digital devices are fine tools for noting something that stirs you. Text yourself or make a file for your observations. In a pinch, I have even called myself and left a voice mail to remind me of something I've seen. Once you begin, you'll get comfortable with reporting on your life and will find that you'll use whatever means are at hand. What this process does not require is an expensive digital recorder, leather notebook, or Cartier pen. That's showing off.

Here's a tip I learned from my husband, a fine former reporter and a really great newspaper editor: Get yourself a pack of inexpensive spiral pocket notebooks, and when you are taking in a landscape—whether emotional or physical—turn that notebook sideways, like a sketchbook. I know how crazy this sounds, but you won't care after you see how effortlessly it signals your subconscious that you're looking for something different. Turn it vertically to report the who, what, when, and where of the topic. Go sideways for the why, where you deepen and broaden your view. Your subconscious loves little cues like this; they help you connect with those screen door slams and childhood survival skills.

Don't think so? Ever notice how distinct smells send you reeling back twenty years or how the way a man wears his hat or sips his tea conjures memories of a long-lost love? It's a do-it-yourself world when writing memoir; we need that screen door of yours to slam just right, and if all it takes is to turn a notebook sideways, I say turn the damn notebook sideways and reap the rewards.

Being hospitable begins with the tools you need for writing what you know—notebooks, pens, and a clean desk—and then paying attention to the goods, the sounds of those porch doors. Next we learn the local customs of writing what you know. In memoir, there are three basic guidelines.

1. Writing Memoir Is About Telling the Truth

Miss Emily Dickinson's Pocket Guide to Writing

But which truth? Whose truth? What about the other person's version? And what, by the way, is the truth?

When you consider the truth, if you try weighing it in your hand or giving it a good look, it doesn't bear up to much scrutiny, if only for the simple fact that there is always someone else's version of it. You say your side is based on the facts. I know. But so does your sister, and according to her, you started it.

How to tell the truth?

Write what you know.

"Here's how I see it" is a powerful phrase to keep in mind, as is "Here's how it happened to me," or "Here's how I felt." Make no claim that your version is the only one. If you do not shoot for the whole truth and nothing but the truth, we're going to get along just fine. Understanding the difference is essential to your success.

And whenever I need some help understanding something, I think of Emily Dickinson, whose rumored inscrutability can really shake up a memoir writer's head.

In poem 1129, she says:

Tell All the Truth but tell it slant—
Success in Circuit lies

What does she mean?

Who *knows*? It's Emily Dickinson. And to make things more slippery, she ends that particular poem with these lines:

The Truth must dazzle gradually
Or every man be blind

And she didn't annotate her work, leaving us to make of it as we want. What I want is to point out the words "slant," "circuit," and "gradually" for you to consider as *Emily's Pocket Guide to Writing*. You could do worse. What we want from you is your take on something, laid out a truth at a time, slowly.

Foremost in memoir, we expect your voice. That's the slant: your take on the world. It's what we're looking for when we buy your book, listen to you on the radio, pay for a magazine that features your essay, or read your blog.

"Circuit" reminds me that I need to make the connections between my ideas quite clear. I've lived these scenes, but you have not, and you won't see how one idea links to the next unless I show you. Keep in mind that your story is deeply embedded in you and so well known to only you that unless you tell it with great care, we will not understand it, no matter how much it dazzles you. Every man will be blind, Emily reminds us, and that's what I see when a sobbing student in my Wednesday night class reads a story while the others look on unmoved. When this happens, it indicates that the piece is still only in the writer's heart and not yet on the page, despite all the typing we see on the sheets before us. So be hospitable to your reader, and provide us with more than the bare-bones facts, foregone conclusions, or mere lists of emotional responses to the events of your life.

Then there's that "gradually," which in practical terms should remind you to open an idea and conclude that idea before moving on, laying one idea after the other slowly, carefully, and deliberately.

Emily has another quote, in poem 318, that nicely sums up how to write memoir:

> *I'll tell you how the Sun rose—*
> *A ribbon at a time—*

She's not inscrutable at all, telling you right there how to tell the truth. Tell me how the sun rose and tell it from your point of view. No matter how caught up you are in your own tale, I'm sure that we can all agree that the sun rises on everyone. Well, that's the way it is with family events, too, when one thing happens to everyone, though no one sees it the same way. Literally universal, the sunrise is something Emily sees in ribbons.

And you?

2. Every Page Must Drive One Single Story Forward

WHAT IS THIS ABOUT?

When I was twenty-two, my mother's mind went to battle with something and lost. It was almost as breathtaking to watch as it was impossible to prevent, and there was no stopping the losses, no quick fix lasting more than a few weeks. It began when my mother's doctor told me that he thought she was becoming senile. I thought she was going mad. We were both wrong.

What I called madness began as forgetfulness—her keys, her phone number—and quickly lunged into severe depression and

memory lapses, confusion, and a halting manner of speaking. Grop-
ing for words, for familiar phrases, she reeled like a semiblind person
in the half-light of dusk. Angry, hostile, violent, incompetent, she
was soon incontinent. She was fifty-one years old when she was diagnosed with Alzheimer's disease, an illness I had never heard of. This
was 1979.

By 1983, I had been at the *New York Times* for six years, having
begun my career there in one of the last classes of copyboys, those
lucky drones who ran around the newsroom all day (or, in my case,
all night), fetching wire copy and delivering it to the appropriate
desk, getting clips from the morgue, coffee from the deli. Having
worked up to the status of news clerk, I pitched the *New York Times
Magazine* editor an idea for a piece on that then-little-known disease. He had not heard of it, nor had his deputy, nor the editor to
whom I was eventually assigned.

In 1983, the magazine published the piece under the headline
"Another Name for Madness." The first first-person account of
Alzheimer's in the mainstream press, it resulted in a contract for a
book, also titled *Another Name for Madness*, with the subtitle "The
Dramatic Story of a Family's Struggle with Alzheimer's Disease."
That subtitle does not read "everything you ever wanted to know
about the Roach family that they know to date, including but not
limited to their immigration to the United States, what they paid for
the houses they lived in, how tall they were then, and, woo-woo, a
peek into the marriage bed of the parents."

No, it does not.

My assignment was very specific, and I nearly lost my mind, living on someone else's money (Houghton Mifflin's) while learning
how to toss out anything that did not illustrate "the dramatic story
of a family's struggle with Alzheimer's disease." And pretty much 99
percent of our lives to date did not.

In the course of reporting the book, I learned a lot about my
mother, researching her life before her illness so that the reader
might fall in love with her before the disease wrenched her away,

attempting to allow the reader to value our loss and, in turn, understand our "dramatic struggle."

At that age, the sum total of facts I knew about my mother could
be pretty much tallied up on just two hands. I knew that she had
been my best friend, my sailing crew, and my tennis partner, and
that she was unhappily married to my father, whom I also adored. It
was a list of details I pretty much shrugged off; it wasn't about me,
after all, and if you'd asked me then to recite it, it would have had
all the emotional zing of a grocery list. I knew only what I needed to
know: that there was a twenty-one-year age gap between my parents,
that when my sister and I were in high school, our mother had gone
back to college and gotten a master's degree in education and then
taught at a bilingual preschool on the Lower East Side of Manhattan when it was still just short of a war zone. A busy kid, I had been
a busier teenager, and then off to college, a busy young woman, not
paying much attention to the chaos of our household, but not miss-
ing that my mother frequently drank too much, and when she did,
she was a nasty woman. That my sister hated her was something I
had known when Margaret moved out the first chance she got and
never looked back.

I had a lot to learn.

And then the phone rang.

A friend of ours called and simply said, "You should know that"—
and then she said a name I knew well—"has just been killed. Call
your mother."

A dutiful young woman, I called my mother at work and waited
a long time while they got her off the playground, and nowhere in
that time did I think about what I was doing or that it was anything
more than what it appeared: that this young man, who was the
brother of my oldest friend and the middle son of our family's close
friends, had just been killed. I stood there in my bare feet with not
very much on my mind.

My mother came to the phone and I told her the news.

"How long have you known?" was her reply.

"About two minutes," I said, thinking her question odd.

"No," she said, "how long have you *known?*"

"Oh," I said, as the facts of twenty-two years recombined themselves: There was that time spent with that other family—all those football games and cocktail parties, overnight trips together, and much later, the moment at my father's funeral when the mother of the dead young man clutched my mother and begged, "Please don't steal my husband"; the nights our mother spent in Manhattan caring for a friend we never met; garish lingerie discovered in a drawer. And I said, "About thirty seconds," and I hung up and called my sister.

"I think Mommy's been having an affair."

"How long have you known?"

The question of the day.

"How long have *you* known?" I asked my sister.

"Since I was nine," said Margaret.

So, what do you do with that? I obsessed over it as I was writing the book. Could we amend the subtitle of that book to be "The dramatic story of a family's struggle with Alzheimer's disease, as evidenced in a wife and mother who lied to her family without anyone but her elder daughter finding out until her dementia made her so sloppy with the details of her life that even the young woman writing this book was forced to notice what she could have known for fourteen years"?

Ah, no.

And then there was how to deal with her drinking. A heavy drinker and a mean drunk, she was also a fascinating, intelligent, compelling, educated, liberal-thinking, hard-voting, snap-witty, gorgeous woman. But when she was drunk, even her beauty became blurred. Alcohol is a brain insult, and since I was writing about a brain disease, I had to deal with it somehow, but the intricacies of being an adult child of an alcoholic were not even vaguely part of the tale I was contracted to write.

So the story was not about a woman who, in her early fifties, was going mad and was simultaneously discovered by her younger daughter to be having an affair, and who was a mean drunk, though I tried like hell to make it about that in the first nine, ten drafts.

Knowing the American public's appetite for sex, I realized that I had to leave out the affair. It would have taken the story off in a direction that would detract from the portrayal of Alzheimer's disease and how it hurtles through a family. The disappointment of having a hard-drinking mother had to be measured: My sister moved home to care for the mother she despised. That's interesting. I did my level best to fall apart. That's interesting, too. Losing different mothers, we had different reactions. That theme stayed in the book.

Will I ever write about her affair? I think I just did.

Her alcoholism? Why? I have nothing to say that's unique, though I've seen the topic done beautifully. Read *Drinking: A Love Story* by the late and great Caroline Knapp. But when Caroline Knapp chose to write another memoir, about the relationship she had with her dog, called *Pack of Two*, she wrote about the same life—hers—with a different answer to the question, "What is this about?"

What I am doing here is the same thing you must do as you write memoir. I am taking inventory of all of my stories, acknowledging that many more exist, while looking for only those that fit this particular assignment. These other stories of my family bulge in the same ways that your stories bulge when you try to tell them. I know I'm not alone in having what we nowadays call a "complicated" family. Not a bit. I also know that my family is no more—or less—complicated than yours. So how do you write about them? By sticking to the story at hand, the one story you have decided to tell, or were assigned to tell, clipping it down on the page as you go, selecting carefully as you type, every day reminding yourself of this one single question: What is this about?

Mine was about "the dramatic story of a family's struggle with Alzheimer's disease." What's yours about?

When first asked this question, beginning writers nearly always say something like "It's about the day I went to the store when I was eight and bought a...," or, "I grew up in the nineteen-fifties, a time of..." and right there I have to cut them off.

What I am asking for is what the tale is about. What they are telling me is how they are going to illustrate the tale. I'm asking for the wrapper, and they are giving me the lozenge. I'm asking for the frame, and they are painting me the picture. I'm asking you to do the same.

What is your story about?

Your answer to this might be something as precise as "revenge." That's manageable. I would argue that something as small as a blog post or a personal essay can be reduced to one word. In all forms of commercial writing—screenplays, fiction, nonfiction, and journalism—this word will appear in what is called "the pitch," the one sentence you use to sell the story to someone else.

So pitch yourself, asking "What is this about?" Perhaps the answer will be "revenge," "mercy," or "betrayal." I would also argue that only one of those three words should ever apply to the story's intent, and that's mercy. It would be impossible to count up just how many people over the years have come into my class hell-bent on writing a revenge tale. So here's some hard-won advice: Never write a story because you want to exact revenge or betray someone. Your story can be about revenge, absolutely, but the story itself should not be wielded as a blunt object, a cat-o'-nine-tails, or a bludgeon. Instead, while writing about the hideous aspects of life, you should attempt to teach us something about the behavior of those involved, about your behavior, about all human behavior. Let us into your story by shedding light on our own dilemmas, fears, happiness, or wide-eyed wonder.

Pretty big requirement, isn't it?

It should be, or else all memoir would be sniveling, and I'm really interested in someone else's sniveling only if it somehow elevates my own. So remember, just like doctors do, "First, do no harm," and don't get suckered into a revenge-to-nowhere tale, where you ask forever how you can get back at someone without ever quite doing so.

Asking the question "What is it about?" will prevent that kind of useless exercise. Ask that, and while the answer might be "revenge," you will end up writing a piece on how you tried to get some, what you learned along the way, or how you plotted and plotted and where that led you.

Writing a tale that seeks revenge, you'll quickly see that tale as merely a list of hurts, which, when you get to the end of that list, is a list that may not interest even you anymore. Revenge as a topic is good; as an intent, it's not. This is another benefit to writing with intent, instead of writing for exercise. Not to go all bumper sticker on you, but learn to write with intent and you might learn something about life—as you will when you learn to reduce the essence of the piece to a single totemic emotion such as "pity" or "joy," a single experience such as "freedom" or "redemption," or even a single phrase such as "the dramatic story of a family's struggle with Alzheimer's disease." That may take some time. But you can do this now: You can decide on a genre—humor, perhaps—and choose how to illustrate it.

Here's how you do it. Say aloud to yourself, "This is a piece of humor, and the illustration is that day at the proctologist," or "This is a tragedy, and the illustration is finding those Polaroids," or "This is about how anger withers the soul, and the illustration is my uncle Henry's struggle for revenge."

What will not work is the phrase "This is a tragedy and the illustration is my marriage." This is too big. On the enormous topic of your marriage, look instead for the moment it shifted—the discovery of the Polaroids that revealed where it is your spouse would rather be; the first time your wife didn't get choked up at someone else's wedding; alone, trying to snap the safety clasp of your bracelet after the death of your partner—and we will see the tragedy. Capture the moment of "aha!" and you'll find one specific story that you can drive forward.

Do you see what is happening here? You are shifting yourself—your story—into a new position of importance, where you are no longer the center of the tale. The story's theme now occupies that place of prominence—the "what is this about" being the main attraction. Look back a few sentences and insert your details into the "this is an (*x*) and the illustration is (*y*)" algorithm, and see how the story is about something and how you, in turn, have become that story's illustration. Understanding this essential shift is the difference between writing good memoir and boring our socks off. And the key to making this shift? Simply accepting that *you* are not the story. Repeat that to yourself: I am not the story. Exactly. You are the illustration. You are the picture in the frame, the lozenge in the wrapper. Get that, and when you do, you will see how your story—the illustration of the theme—gets shifted to the second phrase of this sentence and, by extension, to its proper place.

You are not writing your autobiography when you write memoir, and while entire academic conferences are devoted to howling over the semantic differences, I keep this distinction pretty simple by defining "autobiography" as a book-length depiction of one's entire life and "memoir" as depicting a specific aspect of that life. When students arrive saying they want to write "my memoirs," I'll immediately attempt to redirect that to be "a memoir." I don't always succeed in getting them to boil down their ambitions, though I can say with complete assurance that those who do stand a far better chance of being read by someone else and having those readers enjoy the work.

Want someone to read your stuff? Use the algorithm, and when you do, notice how it makes room for readers. Pretty much (and here comes the howling), if you leave autobiography to the famous, whose highlights we already know and whose details we'd like to have filled in for us, the rest of us can find an audience by writing good memoir. So shift the story's emphasis, and your story will touch on universal themes and—*voilà!*—become of interest to others. This works even if those "others" are an audience of one—for instance, your child—as in, "This is a love story, and the illustration is the moment my adopted daughter was first laid into my arms in China. I am writing it as a letter to her on her tenth birthday," or

"This is about the triumph of hard work, as illustrated by my fifty-year marriage, to be given to my wife on our anniversary."

So ask yourself, "What is this about?" applying that question to one scene, a single event, or a singular appreciation of something in your life.

What is it about? Maybe it's about something as lovely as your new cat and how life got so much better since she came to live with you. Let's map that out, filling in the blanks, using that fine new feline as your illustration.

It is about fulfillment, as illustrated by my relationship with Mittens, as told in a blog post.

Feel that shift?

If you feel like you've been moved off center stage, you have, and you're doing great, since writing memoir is not supposed to be the ego trip that some people make it out to be.

3. Just Because Something Happens, Doesn't Make It Interesting

Your datebook just doesn't cut it here, even if it is Louis Vuitton

Don't believe me? Tell me what you did Tuesday.

"Tuesday morning, I went to the dentist. Oh, he's such a funny man. So funny. I mean, you should go to him. And then, all novocained up, I went shopping. And then I went to lunch and spilled down my front since my mouth was numb, but I went to this new place—it was so fabulous. It was, like, wow. You gotta go."

That's how my friends communicate (no, my friends are no more interesting than yours), and God bless them. Trying to get me to go to their dentist or to a new restaurant, they could tell me what kind of food is served or that the dentist is so homely that he had nothing better to do than pay attention in med school and that he went to Penn. Then I might go. But I'm not going based on this review, because I didn't learn anything. I'm not going to sign up—and that's what reading is: signing up to take a walk with the writer.

The tell-all indicator that a memoir writer is in real trouble is the insistent phrase "But that's how it happened!" Writers who say this while the piece is getting a hard edit from someone else are sinking fast. How it happened is not what makes it interesting. That it happened at all—why it happened and where you go from there—is interesting. Still don't believe me? Tell someone your dreams. Unless you're paying them to listen or haven't slept with them yet, chances are they'll go to some lengths to avoid this download of your subconscious. Try telling your dreams to my husband. He actually gets up and leaves the room if someone attempts to do so. I think that's why we're married—so I don't always have to be the rude one. He'll look at this watch, nod, and actually say, "Oh, look at the time," and *leave*.

When someone says that's the way it happened, I know that the thing is DOA and that the memoir writer could not revive it—in fact, they didn't try. Scenes from real life fade fast, losing blood and paling, and your job is to jump on the damn thing, those wild, electrified Ping-Pong paddles in hand, and jolt it back to life before it goes blue.

How?

By putting it into a context. You have to give readers a reason for this thing to live on in their hearts and minds. Only then can we find your scene lively enough to enjoy, or learn from, or be appalled by. Only then can we laugh at our own family's shenanigans, alter our habits in regards to climate change, or have a transcendent experience by merely reading words on a page. The lamest reason for reading something is because it happened to someone else, and the only real response to that is, "Yeah, so what?"

———

So those are the three rules of memoir. They ask you to tell the truth by making every page drive one story forward and have a context the reader can relate to. Now, the only question is what to write.

THERE'S THE LARGE STUFF, OF COURSE

My steepest and most efficient learning curve was when a kind friend called to ask me to be a columnist in his new magazine. Lovely, I thought, until he said the first assignment was patriotism, one of the prickliest topics of our time. And I thought and thought, and shopped online for about four days, and thought some more, until I remembered my husband's first year as the editor of a newspaper and how much one of us changed during that time.

This was some summers ago in Troy, New York—a scrappy city with all the beauty and history you can get along the mighty Hudson River and with all the issues editors dream about: a nearly devastated economy, civil corruption, and two parades each year in which the newspaper editor gets to ride on a float. The first of these was in June.

My husband, Rex, couldn't wait. He grew up in Rapid City, South Dakota. The drum major of his high school band, he loved a parade.

Me, I had to be out of town that day. And, anyway, the idea of riding a float made me very uncomfortable. I grew up in New York City. *I don't float,* I said to myself. *Don't ask me.* This is what came into focus as I struggled with the piece, and it began to occur to me that real expressions of national pride—much like personal pride—are a comfort we grow into, and perhaps patriotism is not the love-it-or-leave-it choice we were once told it was, but rather the delicatessen plan that most complex issues reveal themselves to be. Maybe now you vote and you sing the national anthem, though you didn't do either in college. Maybe right now you won't float, though maybe someday you will. I started to think that we pick and choose and change as we grow, even on topics as substantial as patriotism and our expressions of it.

Now, you might not know this, but Uncle Sam was a Troy man. Sam Wilson, as he was born, was a meatpacker who supplied troops in the War of 1812, and each year there's a parade in Troy near his birthday, September 13. By the end of our first summer in Troy, my parade comfort level had buoyed to its watershed, and there I was, eyeing a float in South Troy, New York. It was a huge replica of the newspaper my husband edited. We boarded and stood over our names as the pipers, drummers, horn players, fire trucks, clowns, school bands, Girl Scouts, Boy Scouts, and a city on the brink of bankruptcy roared into the united task of honoring Uncle Sam.

The float lurched. There was a bar to hold with one hand. The other hand was for waving.

"What's that?" I shouted, looking down at a box between us.

"Candy," Rex yelled. "We throw it to the crowd."

"We throw it at them?" I shrieked.

"No, we throw it *to* them," he said.

The first gentle toss was delightful. How lovely to watch handfuls of sugary mirth cascade from our perch and to hear the shrieks of children as they scrambled to gather it. How sweet. How like Evita and Imelda and Marie Antoinette all rolled into one.

"I think I'll just wave," I yelled.

I'll float, but I will not toss. I'm not comfortable with it, I remember thinking; it's just not democratic. And it was there, amid my smug reverie on equality, that the attack was launched. We were being bombarded by incoming candy, pelted with our own ammunition, thrown by a suddenly unruly crowd.

"I'm going over," I shouted, grabbing the rail. "Let's go get 'em."

It wasn't the first—or last—time that I have felt the protective hook of my husband's strong fingers in the back of my collar.

Instead, we learned to gauge the crowd block by block—almost person by person—over the three-hour parade route. We figured people on lawn chairs drinking out of paper bags didn't really need any more sweets, for instance. Kids got candy. And while we misjudged a few, we learned that there was no way that the parade-goers were going to behave in any set way and do any one thing—except to celebrate the holiday of a hometown hero. Each individual was bound to respond in his or her own way to the symbols of the day.

And that's pretty much the way America started to look to me as I crafted the essay on the topic of patriotism: one nation, indivisible but comprised of individuals at varying levels of patriotism. And I was comfortable with that and handed in the piece, which ran as written.

So let's apply what we've learned. What is that piece about, and how, if it's something that happened to me, does it become universal? The secret is in that pitch—what you first asked yourself as the piece was begun, what you'd say in class when explaining what you will write, or what you'd tell an editor if offering the piece for publication: It's an essay about patriotism—as illustrated by how one summer, after much debate, I finally climbed aboard a holiday float—to be written for a magazine.

What happens when you pitch yourself a piece on patriotism? What will be your illustration? It might sound like this: It's a piece about patriotism, as illustrated by *y*, to be read on public radio on July Fourth. What's your *y*? Maybe you are French and celebrate Bastille Day; perhaps you are British and Boxing Day is your annual publicly expressed day of unity. St. Patrick's Day? Puerto Rican Commonwealth Constitution Day? Wherever you live, and however you celebrate patriotism, think about those holidays and what you have witnessed, and you will soon identify a personal experience that illustrates that big old theme.

AND THEN THERE'S WHAT'S IN YOUR OWN BACKYARD

Perhaps you want to start the other way around and do not want to begin by choosing a large, cosmic topic. You just want to start writing and see where it goes. You bet. Let's do it that way. Maybe you'd like to introduce your children to their dead relatives. It's easier than it sounds.

A recent student of mine wrote a fine book based on the lovely argument that all of her children take after relatives and friends they had never known, that her children's gestures and habits, tastes and preferences, were first acquired by her, via these now long-gone loved ones, and passed along to her offspring. In her book, she successfully introduced these individuals to one another, making only enough copies for each child, giving it to them at the holidays.

So let's pick a dead relative—say, your maternal grandmother. Now let's choose a scene in which to illustrate who she was in the lineage of your loving family. That might be best illustrated in how she taught you to bake cupcakes when you were five years old. For this, the reader needs to see if she measured her ingredients, wiped her hands, washed those hands, or if she washed your little hands inside hers. These are the details that truly illustrate her, characterizing for the reader who she is, who she is to you, and, by extension, what the piece is about. What the reader does not need to know is her height and weight, or if her eyes were brown—unless, of course, those eyes oh-so-piquantly matched the shade of the chocolate frosting. The details we need to know reveal her care with those she loved; the others are mere descriptions and hold no weight. And as scary as it may sound, when we talk cooking and eating, we are talking love, since the entire history of how a family loves—where and how they learned to love—can be told in most kitchens.

And when I say that in class, someone always shoots up her hand.

"Yeah, well, my grandmother didn't teach me to bake. My grandmother was a drunk."

Did she instead teach you how to make the perfect martini? Did you grow up in a household like mine, where gin-soaked cocktail onions and olives were considered sufficient dinner vegetables for children? Did you teach yourself to bake? Does that reflect how your family either withholds emotion or expresses love? And when you went home with your college roommate for Christmas and her whole blond family moored itself around the granite island in their Greenwich, Connecticut, kitchen to ice holiday cupcakes, just how many of them did you cram into your mouth, trying to fill up that gaping hole in your heart?

Do you remember? If so, you're good to go. So start writing, and as you set down the details, you'll see universal themes percolate to the surface. Choose one, plug it in, and then toss out any scenes or details that do not illustrate that chosen *x*. That's the beauty of that little algorithm; it will do its work for you no matter which variable you choose first. So use it.

HERE WE GO

My class runs for six weeks, once a week for three hours. On the first night I'll ask for the topic the students will write as one essay, told in first person at fewer than 750 words. As I go around the room, invariably each subject is too big, almost everyone saying something like, "Gender. Being a sensitive man who came of age in America in the 1970s, I'm very sensitive to this idea of gender."

Uh-oh.

Or: "My great-grandparents."

Hmmm.

These proposed topics must be shrunk, or that writer will not come back, having failed to wrestle onto the page a monster of unmanageable heft. We'll use that writing algorithm to boil down these both vague and enormous ideas into moments illustrating what the writer is truly after. Maybe Gender Guy is really quite *un*comfortable on the sensitive topic of our true selves and can recall the exact moment when things got slippery.

Those "aha!" moments in life are complex and interesting to others, certainly more so than a screed on the gender sensitivity of any one man.

Boiling down great-grandparents is a cinch, and I'll ask questions until the writer sees a moment when perhaps her ancestors' tale can be told in the dab on the nose with some cupcake icing or on the head of the inherited hatpin she gave her own daughter to defend herself on the New York City subway.

Right around the fourth or fifth person I get to, someone will inevitably offer up the topic "My rat bastard boyfriend who just left," and I know we're making real progress.

"What did he take when he went?" I'll ask.

Because when people leave us, what they take tells us if they are going for good, going for show, or merely slinking off to someone else. Saltshakers are a good indication that the boyfriend has not got someone else lined up. Taking only a sandwich tells us that he's hungry and that he has little more than tonight in mind.

We all know what he takes when he's leaving for good, because it has happened to us, and it is in the list of what he took that the tale is told. That's what makes the story truthful, as well as what makes it yours: What did he take of yours, what of his, and how do you define those, divide those, when at one time those lines were blurred by the smudge of love?

I've been teaching for thirteen years, to more than 800 students to date, in classrooms and online, and in nearly every class I've taught, we get some kind of list of what someone took on the way out. But people leave in different ways. Among the memorable lists I've read was one by a woman who turned in fifteen slender sentences, divided into three categories: "What I took," "What I heard," and "What I said." The piece needed nothing more—no preamble, no introduction—for us to understand that it was a list of what she took with her, what she heard, and what she said at the bedside of her best friend as she died.

No one who reads it is unchanged by that list.

READ IT IN THE WANT ADS, SEE IT IN THE CARDS

How wild can you get? Can you tell your story in the form of a want ad? Absolutely. How about relating the demise of a marriage by listing the ingredients that once defined that union but when seen in hindsight provide a recipe for disaster? If you do, you'll quickly learn to tell things lean, jumping ahead of every other blogger and essay writer by mastering how to tell your tale succinctly from the proverbial get-go.

Writing is a form of packing, and you always want to be on the move, so packing light should be the ethic, no matter the length of the piece. And while this is hard to grasp, keep it in mind. Pack light. We're not embarking on a cruise for a year, or even going on a weekend trip. A blog post, a personal essay, even a full-length memoir, is not about stuffing in as much as you can; rather, it's about illustrating something correctly. No matter how many words it is, the piece is just a day trip with someone listening in—the reader. You are not writing the history of the world, or even your world. Wanting to be heard, the temptation is to go big and throw in everything we think we might need. But it's a mistake. And so we must unpack, casting off all nonessentials and, along the way, learning what to leave out.

This ethic is beautifully expressed in what Michelangelo reportedly said about his sculpture: that the form lived in that piece of marble, and the artist's job was to chip down to find it. So it is with your story, from which you must doggedly chip away the entire history of everything, to only one small tale, after which there will be a whole lot more left behind than what we'll see before us.

To illustrate this, think of memoir as laying out only a few cards from an entire deck, one at a time, each card moving forward the one story you choose to tell. Ever seen the tarot read? Writing memoir is a little like that—all you can supply yourself with is what fits in the hand. All the readers see is what you lay down. This is particularly difficult when the topic is you. Ego being what it is, when given permission to write about ourselves, we tend to spill all those things we've done, thoughts we've had, and people we've known, since they all seem wildly important. And they are. To *us*, though not necessarily to *them*, those other people, the readers.

Appreciating the difference between the personal tale and its value and the universal tale and its appeal is hard-won. I see this value proposition in action whenever I visit my friend Dan, whose antiquarian bookstore is among the loveliest spots on earth. Perfectly placed in the Berkshire foothills, the building was once a general store and now houses thousands of old books, most of which he acquires from strangers. People frequently bring in their beloved childhood books to sell, cradling their edition of *Winnie the Pooh*, *Kidnapped*, or *Catcher in the Rye*, genuinely believing that these editions are of value. And they are, Dan always says kindly—to them. But it is only the first editions or rare editions—those books that have market value—that are attractive to him, as he explains countless times each year to people whose books he must decline.

It's the same with your own tale. Of course it's of value to you, but how are you going to make it of value to me as well? Here's how: Make it small. Make it rare. Make it a first for me as a reader, and I'll remember it forever. Make it of value to someone else, even if—actually, no, *especially* if—those intended readers are your family. What could be more important than that? Or, as I've learned, more difficult?

Which is why I use the medium of the personal essay to teach memoir of any length. It is quite simply the greatest, fastest method to learn to pack light. At about 750 words, a personal essay gives the writer more than enough space to tell one tale from her point of view. But it's hard work. Writing a personal essay takes discipline, evoking another great dictum of art: You must learn to draw before you can learn to paint. Essays require the same kind of control as drawing, and control is all about choosing what to put in or leave out. And while writers seem to want to tell their story, few understand that it must be told one illustrative scene at a time. The A.C. Moore and Michaels craft store aisles are packed with folks gluing down and sequining up their entire lives' stories; they'd be far more satisfied writing down one life event—one graduation, wedding, or funeral—and sharing it.

So here's some good news, perhaps the best news of all, learned while reading the powerful book *The War of Art*, in which Steven Pressfield reminds us that all real athletes learn to "play hurt." By this he means that they go out and do their jobs, even when injured. The phrase actually made me weep, so profound is its application to memoirists. Reading it for the first time, I actually closed the book and held it to my chest. Here's how it applies to us: People frequently tell me that they fully intend to write a piece of memoir just as soon as they understand the meaning of their lives. Longing to do so, these potential writers suffer needlessly, since the marvelous truth is that you can take on life in bits, at any age, under any circumstances. To write a compelling essay, you need merely to be amazed by how, when explaining intimacy to your adolescent child, you gained some quiet understanding of your own sexuality; or when it is you became comfortable with the fact that much of marriage is pantomime, where looking interested and making the gestures of engaged listening are good enough to get you both through to the next day. Wait to "understand" adolescents or marriage and you'll never, ever write. Mere flashes are all the understanding you need bring to the writing table.

Because when you have a flash of understanding on one topic, you can write an essay. Write an essay and you tackle a scene. Master the scene and you can write seventy-five of them and have yourself a book. And here's an unexpected dividend: Write a book about an aspect of your life and you might gain perspective, since just as in living, success in writing is all about which details you choose to emphasize.

READY OR NOT

On that first night of class, as the students relate vivid scenes they want to write—the very ones we'll prune down to a writable size—my hope is that everyone begins not only to recognize which stories might work, but also which are not yet ready for mining.

At some point in the class, I'll tell the students about a male architect I barely knew when he married a friend of mine. For their wedding, he not only designed but also sewed his wife's crushed white velvet, floor-length, cut-on-the-bias wedding dress and made her a white pillbox hat to match.

Consider that scene for a moment: another bride, another groom, another musty old church filled with people in their thirties marveling at this Olympiad of sewing, the guests shooting wide-eyed looks at one another. Here comes the bride. And that groom in the designer tux and slender Italian eyeglasses—is he straight or what? Great scene, but that illustration—the crushed velvet wedding dress, the tall groom, whispers rocketing around the stone church—needs a context, a wrapper, to evolve beyond being a toast at the couple's twentieth anniversary.

What is the wedding story about? I have no idea, though in the years since I delighted in witnessing it (and their happy marriage), I have picked it up a thousand times and had a look, each time putting it away again. I couldn't pitch it because I did not know what it's about; specifically, I did not know what it illustrated. Gorgeous, it's been patiently waiting for me to find a place where it makes sense, in context. I think I just did.

I've got a million of them, thank God. And so do you.

Chapter 2

Galileo in Wal-Mart

MY CLASS IS called Writing What You Know. Based on that simple adage to "write what you know," the message tucked into the course title is complex and requires nothing less than chucking the big bang notion of reality TV, talk radio, and many best-selling memoirs, and instead learning to go small.

It's in the small moments that life is truly lived. Lessons from the "large moments" are hard to absorb and rarely learned. Consider a quarreling couple coming back together. Only in movies does the lavish trip to Paris or the über-bracelet rejoin an exhausted pair of people. In real life, one night someone laughs again at another's joke, another passes the peas and includes a touch of fingertips, and life together begins again.

Not long ago, *Martha Stewart Living* sent me to Ann Arbor, Michigan, to interview Janice Longone, the first designated Curator of American Culinary History. This is someone who relates human history through an ice cube—or a bag of coffee beans, tea leaves, or salt—using edible vehicles to roll out our tale. The kind of person writers need in their lives, she makes you think outside prescribed methods of narration.

In the basement of the William L. Clements Library at the University of Michigan–Ann Arbor, we looked over a mere handful of the more than 20,000 items—including books, menus, magazines, and advertisements—she had recently donated. Among the most comprehensive private collections of such material, it represents "enough material for fifteen hundred PhDs," she said, while regarding an intricate early-twentieth-century menu and dropping into our chat the word "realia."

"What is that?" I asked, rolling the word around to nail its tricky pronunciation—re-A-lee-ah.

"Small stuff. Collectibles. Isn't it a lovely word?"

It is.

This ethic—the small stuff, the true collectibles, realia—is how to tell the tale. Simplicity succeeds, especially amid the current memoir craze of outing our outré families.

There are many over-the-top memoirs on the market, and while several are bestsellers, I'd argue that sometimes the people writing them are invested in another kind of success altogether. Sure, they learned to type, but they haven't learned to value the reader, whose hunger for the truth is enormous and whose thirst for understanding this life is unquenchable.

This my-life-is-crazier-than-yours-could-ever-be mentality is also why so many badass, lying memoirs have made it to the shelves: The writers simply told us what they thought we wanted to hear. They were wrong. I don't want to be lied to. I want to be told the truth so I can negotiate this life with some degree of accuracy and honor. For that we need to look to the small moments.

Faced with the assignment to write the truth, some people lie like dogs because they think the truth pales. How very sad. For me, it is never pale. I'm far more interested in a revelation after one night in jail than in any transcendent awareness cooked up after three months in the slammer. And I'm not alone. Most of us are more likely to do one night in jail than some serious hard time. James Frey's memoir, *A Million Little Pieces*, staked the false claim of truths learned after months in prison, distancing the truth from readers, in essence saying, "You can have this kind of truth only if you have this kind of life," which is nonsense. Transcendent revelation can occur eating Girl Scout cookies, if your head's in the right place.

And your head is in the right place—that is, if you keep your eyes open. Do so, and you may be amazed. And humbled. You might giggle more. And you'll write better.

I'm not out in the world actively mining for transcendent moments. I'm an American from Queens, New York, who possesses little more than a patchwork, sandlot sense of the divine. I am no more Zen, enlightened, or realized than the next person, stumbling into and through little moments of realization. But I do catch some of those moments in my notebook or on my handy index cards. What frequently happens to me is that some odd aspect of an encounter amuses or disturbs me, and when I'm in my car or walking home, I'll jot down one image, or piece of conversation, which I'll start to think about and worry like a set of prayer beads. *What was that I just saw?* I'll ask myself. *What just happened there?* Like those after-bubbles from a camera flash, they'll stick around only so long, so I write them down, having learned that what at first might seem tangential frequently expands upon consideration.

This kind of thinking is usually discouraged, of course. It seems frivolous. Or weird. Or outright hostile. So be discreet. Don't slap down your notebook on the Thanksgiving table and announce, "Okay, folks, this year everything is on the record." Instead, between courses, merely jot down an image or two. We are well trained to attend and pay attention to the big stuff—birthdays, holidays, graduations—so while you're there, look for the small things. I'm quite sure that some of your best work will come from allowing the odd details of life to provoke you.

Here's an example, set on the evening that my neighbor's dog died. A big event, absolutely, and unforgettable, though what I wrote down when I arrived home was none of the regular fragments of experience—the who, what, when—but merely a description of an article of clothing someone was wearing that night.

There had once been a time when our dogs divided us. It happens in neighborhoods, and it did in ours. Each of us lived behind our own invisible electric fence, keeping our dogs in our own territories, allowing for no mixing of our pedigreed charges. The humans walked, we waved, but we knew little of one another's lives, except, perhaps, that it was the woman in each home who walked the dog. That much was clear. And for a while that's how it was: Not much contact, little to say, we walked our dogs along the perimeter of each other's lives.

We became aware of changes in our homes only via a husband's obituary in the newspaper, the absence of the truck in another's driveway, the vision of one of us walking without a dog but crying. Small inquiries at the hem of the yard, nods exchanged, solace offered, we edged closer. A new dog appeared; there is always something to say about a puppy. Always.

Then, as that puppy grew and neared his third birthday, he got very sick and nearly died from something, it seemed, that a neighbor's dog had survived only the week before. She, too, had nearly died, and the exchanges and the information, cards, a bouquet, a note, and longer conversations ensued.

What we talked about when we talked about our dogs, of course, was love.

And then one summer evening came a pounding on my front door.

"Marion! Marion!" I heard as I was making an upstairs bed.

"Marion!"

My dog and I went running to find my neighbor. Smeared with dirt and tears, having come in from hours of gardening, she had just found her beloved dog motionless on the kitchen floor.

Oh no, I thought. *Oh no.*

Soon we were standing over the peaceful body of her hulking animal, all 140 pounds of him. He seemed asleep. He was not. And as we knelt and stroked him, a car door slammed outside and I went out to see the other woman in our dog-friend-triangle coming up the driveway. But something was odd. *My*, I thought, *how thin she is. How thin.* Or something. Maybe that's not it. But there was some aspect of the equation of her body size that was off. Just one of those snatched thoughts you get under pressure, the very thinking collapsing as I saw that she, too, was in tears.

And then there were three of us standing over the ten-year-old body of the dog we had known since he was all ears and paws.

Others arrived to help. There were plans made and calls made, and for thirty minutes or so there was a lot of action, and then for an instant, it was again just us three in the kitchen.

We were going to take the body to the local animal hospital for cremation. Not even we could dig a hole this big, though I know that for an instant we considered it. Keeping him close. Keeping him home. But no.

And then, as we began to pile into cars, came the question.

"Do I look like shit?" This, from the woman whose dog had just died.

Only a woman would ask.

And only two such friends would think before they replied. She had been gardening most of the day, on her knees, in the dirt. She had been crying. It was hot. We all looked like shit. But what do you say to move forward a woman who needs to go say good-bye to her dog? How do you not lie and yet get her onward into the place she needs to go? How to be tender, yet prodding?

I hadn't needed to debate this, as the other of us had this clearly covered, gently touching the voluminous shorts I now saw that had been the reason she looked so thin, so fragile, at first.

And then came the gift.

"I'm wearing my dead husband's swimming trunks. I think we're good."

And I snorted. And the woman who just lost her dog belted out a laugh, a laugh so big that it propelled us where we needed to go next.

In this case, it had been the bathing trunks that had provoked me, noticed and tucked away amid the sadness and the heat. It was those shorts I carried home in my head—like a burr in a sweater, a sand particle in an oyster—and after I wrote down "swimming trunks," they did their job to irritate me just enough to see their larger theme. It's the little stuff that matters. Never disrespect its power.

A dead giveaway that someone is disparaging the truth is that cool kind of cynicism that voices many memoirs. No writer should aspire to being too cool to care about the small stuff. Doing so is an offense to us all. The great A. J. Liebling addresses the crime beautifully, reminding us, "Cynicism is often the shamefaced product of inexperience."

Brush up on your Shakespeare

Lying also happens when writers do not know what to say. So do some research. Writing what you know does not mean you don't check your facts. Accuracy counts. Memoir demands fact-checking, since memory, by its very definition, is subjective.

Have reference books nearby at all times, including the following:

- A good modern dictionary
- *Roget's Thesaurus.* We will not even discuss using the one on your computer, except to say that it's forbidden.
- *Bartlett's Familiar Quotations*
- A rhyming dictionary
- The Bible
- A book of days, referencing famous things that happened on various dates
- *The Complete Shakespeare*
- Several standard texts of language usage, such as *The Elements of Style* by Strunk and White, and *The Elements of Grammar* by Margaret Shertzer, *The Chicago Manual of Style*, and *The New York Times Manual of Style and Usage*
- A word and phrase origins book
- A dictionary of symbolism
- One up-to-date, and one hopelessly out-of-date, atlas (country names change)

- Any other old damn thing you want. A full twenty-four-volume standard encyclopedia is nearby for me, as are horticultural encyclopedias; a complete set of field guides to bugs, birds, plants, and mammals; several books on how things work and how they were invented and the like; as well as my copy of *The Complete Poems of Emily Dickinson* and *The War of Art* by Steven Pressfield, either of which I open at random every time I think about getting up from my office chair before the piece is done.

If you're working in a library, you're all set. They have all of these. If you're at home, buy them used from any reputable online book dealer, like alibris.com or ABEbooks.com. Without them, you will make things up or get stuck, and there is never any reason to get stuck.

THE MYTH OF WRITER'S BLOCK

Writer's block has been immortalized in story and in no fewer than thirty-three movies, and is the threat lurking behind every time-sucking exercise and writing prompt. And by the way, you've got writer's block if you are merely exercising and not writing with intent. And if you don't, you will; I've seen people so sure they cannot give up their preassigned, writing-book-provided prompts that they shake, making me think writer's block is the new crack. Either way, just say no. Say the hell with it and do some research.

The inability to move forward melts when you open a reference book. Don't believe me? Veterans Day is a yearly event, and I've never met anyone who does not have some response to war. You could write up yours for your local newspaper or local radio station. Begin by looking up "courage," "valor," or "veteran" in the dictionary; read quotes on it in *Bartlett's*, or paw through *Roget's Thesaurus*, and the piece will split wide open.

Determined to get that letter to your daughter finished this year in time for her birthday, or that anniversary gift written for your spouse? Both are great intents. So get out the family photo album, plant it on your desk, and use it like the reference book it is. Literally refer to it, and write about what you see.

Other, deeply personal books work as well, including diaries, recipe files, and, of course, yearbooks. I knit and keep a photo journal of every sweater/hat/sock, who it was for, the date it was begun, and when it was delivered, and only recently realized the journal's value as a reference. In it, I am reminded that a favorite piece of clothing is named my "Gulf War" sweater, knit when watching war on live television was still a novelty but so upsetting that I had to keep my hands busy. The photo caption for "Lillian's funeral sweater" reveals that the casting on began as we departed for my mother-in-law's burial in Indiana and how the last button was attached eight days later, when pulling back into our driveway. If I can locate a theme in there—and I think I can—I could write a memoir from this journal and never get blocked.

Research also includes other people, since no one invested in your success will permit you to not write. For this, I have Margaret, my older sister. We are both writers, and neither one of us lets the other stay blocked for more than a few moments. So, to borrow a phrase from our national TV mentality, use one of those lifelines and call for help.

Here's how it recently went for us.

"Margaret?"

"Yes."

"What was the name of the boy who rode the bus with me every day to school?"

"You mean your imaginary friend or the real children, Marion?"

Ooooh. Nasty. I like it. That got me going. I never knew she thought I had imaginary friends. That's good for four topics: my imaginary friends; my daughters' imaginary friends; what my sister and I don't know about each other; the she said/she said of sisterhood. Think of writer's block as matter, hit it with the right hammer (your sister's intolerance for not writing), and it smashes into a bazillion molecules called ideas—all small, all writable, all uniquely yours.

Two weeks later.

"Margaret?"

"Yes?"

"Were those blue-sashed Christmas dresses Grandma made us from the drapes?"

"Those were *Easter* dresses, Marion. And, Marion, that was Scarlett O'Hara who had dresses made from drapes. Not you."

Smash. There in the rubble I see love in the guise of a grandmother's sewing; the motivational force of a sister's exasperation; my long-standing misassociation with Scarlett, all of which need only a frame.

Sometime later:

"Margaret, what's your favorite flavor of ice cream?" I asked this in an e-mail, wanting to write a post for our shared blog, figuring us split down the chocolate/vanilla divide.

Well, that started something. Apparently she doesn't like ice cream and used that invitation to write this in reply:

Ice Cream

I just wanted ice cream, a Good Humor bar to be precise, either Toasted Almond with its crunchy, pebbled exterior, or perhaps a smooth, slippery Creamsicle to gradually whittle down with the warmth of my tongue: licking, licking, trying to stay one lick ahead of meltdown.

Buying ice cream from the hulking white cube of a truck was one ritual of long summer days in my 1960s suburbia, as much as playing outside until supper, or the volatile smell of charcoal-lighter fluid splashing in an arc onto the nightly pyramid of black briquettes. The adults had their happy hour; we had our Good Humor.

Where Mommy was at this moment on this particular evening I do not recall, but no matter. Her long red clutch purse was on the Victorian chaise in the master bedroom, the room she shared with my father. It was furnished with the suite of his-and-hers dressers and twin beds pushed together into one faux expanse, but with that tricky, insistent abyss down the middle where they joined, the one you could fall into. Sometimes we roughhoused in there, my younger sister and I, two giggling, squealing girls in pigtails, and down the crack between Mommy's side of things and Daddy's, one or the other of us would go, disappearing.

But this early summer evening I am on my own in the ballroom-sized space with its crystal chandelier and matching sconces, the floor-length draperies and upholstery all in pale green raw silk. The way I remember it, I am nine, and I want ice cream, and I can hear the bells of the ice-cream truck growing louder, so there is no time to find anyone grown up and ask for the money I need.

I am on what to a nine-year-old is a mission: seeking the shortest route to getting my immediate needs met. Give me ice cream now.

I race upstairs, two steps at a time, to that familiar room where the people whose job it is to protect me start and end their day under matching nubby, dark green bedspreads. I go and reach my small hand into that big red wallet to find the dollar, as I have in my nine-year-old innocence so many times before. Give me ice cream now.

The bells ring again, and I dig deeper into the clutch—Why is there no single?—and then my hungry rummaging goes really wrong.

I do not find the currency to end my craving, but instead an end to untroubled summer evenings where scoring a dollar bill in Mommy's wallet was my most urgent desire. In my hand is a small black-and-white photo of the man who is perhaps my father's closest friend, the father of my sister's closest friend, the man with whose wife and family we go to dinner routinely and even travel with sometimes.

I don't, and I do, understand.

What follows is not the treat I seek, but (to state the obvious, and say it tritely) an end of innocence. I have not even had a boyfriend yet; I don't wear (or need) a bra—and won't for years to come. I am a child, with a girl's white cotton undershirt and Carter's Spanky Pants beneath the pedal pushers and striped top Mommy bought me; my white mercerized cotton socks are folded over carefully at the ankles. I am a child, but at this instant I am a child who is forced to become the Confronter, a place in the family achieved when hand touched photo. *Tag: You're it.* No longer someone searching for a dollar, I began my life's search for an honest answer, no matter how ugly. And I begin a lifetime habit of asking questions, endless questions, the first of them spoken silently to myself there in that bedroom.

"Why is there a picture of Jack in Mommy's wallet?" I was not silent for long.

The answers—from Mommy, from Daddy, and even from Marion—were always the same, no matter how I phrased my question: Be quiet, they'd say, in one form or another. Don't talk that way. Be quiet.

Does Margaret's version of the same family experience temper mine? No. Does hers differ wildly from my version? Yes. She found out about our mother's affair when she was nine, after all. Does this make for a very different narrative sister-to-sister? Oh, baby, does it ever. Is one of us wrong? Ah, no. Should another version of the same family moment leave you blocked? Never.

USE THE MUSE YOU'VE GOT

My husband claims that I don't know how to feel about him until I write it down. That's fair. I frequently don't know how I feel about something or someone until I consider it and get past my "I like this" initial reaction to all of life, including my spouse.

The fodder for columns, essays, blog posts, and parts of one of my books, my husband is the cool palm on my hotheaded ways, which is a much better characterization of our marriage than writing "my husband loves me very much." How would I further illustrate that? I might grab some funny recent moment and begin asking myself, "What is this about?"

I recently awoke to see the words "Menopause made me do it" scribbled on a shard of paper laid on my nightstand. A 4:00 a.m. thought. Seeing it, I began to build a piece based on an event the day before.

Riding in the car, my husband and I were merely zipping along during a rare time alone. No one was overcaffeinated; everyone was sober. It was a lazy afternoon all around. Relaxed, and with no deadlines, we were going to our favorite bicycle store to see what was new.

A car zipped by with one of those oval stickers on the bumper portraying merely a number. Have you wondered what they mean? I have. Those little oval stickers used to mean only that someone had touristed in some European city, perhaps even purchased there the vehicle they are now driving and proudly want to display that. Then those little oval stick-ons started to mean more (or less) than that, and I got confused.

The sticker on the car read "70.3." Nothing more.

And as we drew closer, I gave no time to the fairly sane man whose job in life it has become to reel me in. Instead, before asking what the sticker could possibly mean, I stuck my head out the window and yelled, "Thirty-eight Double D!"

You know that feeling? Maybe cats feel this way after hurling a hairball. I hope so.

My husband was silent for a moment; the look on his face was the one he gets when he is forced to quickly shove together the evidence before him into some narrative he can live with. He looked at the bumper sticker. He looked at me. And then he began to laugh in that way I have come to value as the ultimate paycheck of my life. If marriage is the hardest room to work in Vegas—and it is—at that moment all the slots were pouring out in my bucket as he laughed and laughed and laughed.

When he was finally able to speak, he calmly asked, "You don't know what those are, do you?"

"Nope."

"Triathlons. Half Iron Man competitions. Those are the distances the people have gone."

"Huh."

Now I know.

I knew, too, that was not a radio essay, but rather a blog post, something with a compact message that many women online want to read. So I published it on my blog. And my husband doesn't mind a bit, since I never air my laundry, sticking merely to writing about my bras. Knowing the difference requires understanding how to choose what to write.

Focusing your lens

Consider Galileo in Wal-Mart. Imagine the master standing amid the deep fryers, digital cameras, and lawn chairs. All he wants is the one small part he needs to perfect the telescope. Then he'll prove that the earth revolves around the sun, and not the other way around, as was the standard message of the church in his time. Seeking a small item to prove a big theory, Galileo must not get distracted by the Christmas icicle lights and stainless-steel slow cookers, the ionized hairdryers and six-time-zone watches. He must go into Wal-Mart, get only what he needs, and come back out. Then he'll convince us to see the universe the way he does.

Yours is the same assignment. You must speed-shop your over-stocked whiz-bang subconscious, snagging only those items tagged by the subject you've chosen, leaving all those other pretty, shiny, digital, marked-down objects on the shelves. It's as though you must carry a custom-made magnet, attracting merely the smallest, precisely charged metal shavings. This is not easy. But mastering the skill of a good quick grab is essential to your success.

This may be how Elton John once thought of dressing for his concerts, wearing those custom-made glasses that accessorized every outfit; in your case, it's a tailored pair of lenses through which to choose only those items you need to tell a precise tale. Each tale, of course, requires a new set of shades.

After all, if life is lived in the small moments, you're going to have a whole lot of stuff to sift through to illustrate your big point, which is precisely why most people write badly about the big events, typing sentences like "It was the saddest I ever remember" or "I'll never forget the day that…"

Even in life's big experiences—birth and death being the top two—how we live consists of individual moments in which we can find some truths. Consider a recent funeral and how you'd write it. To hook me, you must display how it moved you, honoring the great journalism tradition: "Show, don't tell." Don't tell me it was sad; show me how sadness looks, and let me do the math.

"Oh," I should say to myself at the end of your piece, "now *that's* sad."

Why not write about dressing for the last rite, or undressing after the event, shedding the clothing and accessories you needed to power you through the dreadful day? Given the choice of sitting at a funeral and dressing for one, I'll bet the ranch house on the second essay any day. Anyone can sit through a funeral. But while we zip up the dress before or unclasp the pearls after, there's a moment to witness—another human being preparing for or coming off of the universal big stuff of life. And that is made up of exacting detail.

Maybe the story is best told by what someone else wore, and as I type that, what slams aside all other images in my head is my friend at the funeral of her teenage daughter. Shock was not what I registered when rounding the terrible corner from parlor to funeral home viewing room, and I saw the mother shrouded in a filthy ski jacket and tattered pants, draped over her child's closed casket. Relaying her clothes relays the emotion: The sadness is stitched into the detail about the jacket.

That's what it looks like when someone tries to stop time, when time stops for only one person, or how we appear when we attempt to refuse to go on. Which is it exactly? Depends on how you write it, but the details are a far more penetrating way to deliver the topic of the saddest day of your life than by telling me it was the saddest day of your life. These were the clothes she had been wearing two days earlier, when she was told that her daughter had been hit by a train. What are you going to do with that?

When his wife was dying, the great C. S. Lewis wrote that he had "no idea that grief felt so much like fear." When my mother was careening through our lives with her Alzheimer's, I wrote, "Grief is a mute sense of panic." How would you write it? What did you wear? Ilene Beckerman took this concept and, in 164 pages, created *Love, Loss, and What I Wore*—a major bestseller, published in 1995, that is now a play.

Small moments. I learned this when a student who both hated and worshipped her brawling, drunken, Irish Catholic father read her first piece aloud to our class. She wrote over and over and over how she hated and loved him, despised and adored him, without once showing what that might look like. We learned nothing except that she was conflicted.

I asked her what she does for Father's Day, if she sends a card. Howling with laughter shot full of rue, she spat back that every year she goes to card shops, coming home empty-handed. Father's Day was coming up, and I suggested she go to the card store, notebook in hand, and report the piece. She did, and it was marvelous.

And that incident reminded me, too, of how much the Gregorian calendar is a memoir writer's right-hand man.

THINK IN PROPINQUITIES

Use the calendar. Even if you are planning to read your piece at the Seder table or at Christmas dinner and are not considering mass-market publication, writing things well in advance of high emotional holy days is one fine way to learn to write with intent. Get a stockpile of ideas and, if you want to publish, resolve this time to write and then send them out in a timely manner (weeks in advance) to your local public radio station or to the magazine (six months to a year in advance) you read regularly. Have a backlog to publish on your blog. Act as if you're on deadline.

These high emotional holy days of the year are many. Some are widely celebrated—Christmas, Hanukkah, Thanksgiving. Some are deeply personal—anniversaries, birthdays. Others are both universal and deeply personal, such as the summer camp season and the beginning and end of each school year.

But this far into this book, you know better than to write a turkey-and-relish piece for Thanksgiving. Remember the small? The wrapper and the lozenge? Look amid your overstocked shelves. Think gratitude or taking stock; think of the background emotional stuff instead of Norman Rockwell's steaming bird; think of the infinitesimal ways in which we are taught gratitude; look up "gratitude" in the thesaurus.

This is thinking in propinquities. It's an angle shot. If the day on which you want the essay to air or the blog post to be published is Thanksgiving, don't give us a photograph of the day, but rather a sidelong glance at how you learned new ways to be grateful.

Try thinking of the traditional holiday gathering as the background of your piece, in front of which you will set your drama. This is the same device illustrated earlier with the story about the power of the sisterhood set at the death of my neighbor's dog. This time, the scenery is a beloved national holiday. Thinking of Thanksgiving as the setting, rather than the subject, will release you from the literal "but that is the way it happened" point of view and will make way for some universal themes—grace, bounty, plenty—to peek through, allowing you to see what your story is about. You can show us the wonder of the small—the realia—comfortably set in a surrounding we all recognize. Did you ever get a bit steamed over the smooth or chunky cranberry sauce debate? No? Really? Well, good for you. We always did, and in there is a piece to be written about letting things go. Or not letting things go. Or, perhaps, about compromise.

Consider your myriad family holidays. At which of those did you learn a little something, have a small awakening, or even a moment of trancendence?

When I ask myself this question, this is what comes up:

I was single, living in Manhattan, but on that Thanksgiving it was a particularly unglamorous life. With a snapped ankle, a cast, and crutches, I thought that no holiday cheer was worth cantilevering the flights of stairs from my brownstone apartment. Then the phone rang.

My hostess was insistent. Her son would come into Manhattan and fetch me. I couldn't let him. And I couldn't say no. Through the decade it took to lose my mother to Alzheimer's, these were the only people who invited us to holiday dinners each year. And now it would be my first holiday alone.

No, I'd get there, I promised. I'd take a cab.

The only thing in my fridge worth bringing was a six-pack of imported beer. Into a bag over my shoulder it went, and balanced on my crutches, facing uptown traffic, I felt like little more than a grimace in a skirt. Especially as cab after cab sped away without me after finding out I was going to Queens—not a short trip. If I'd had a lonelier hour in New York I don't remember it.

Finally slumped into a backseat, I wept across the Triborough Bridge. At Shea Stadium, things got sluggish in the holiday traffic.

After a while, I looked at the photo on the cabbie license and realized the driver was probably about my age. We were going nowhere and the silence was awkward. We sat, stopped, not moving at all. I knew he'd rather be in Manhattan, making the fares. I reached into the bag I was carrying and offered him a beer, and we sat in the traffic by Flushing Bay for more than an hour, having our holiday drink, talking. An actor, without family, far away from home, he had volunteered to work the holiday so other cabbies could be off. When we finally got to

Queens, ninety minutes later than I was expected, my friends swarmed out the door, fearing, I guess, for what had happened to me.

"You have to come in," said my host to the cabdriver.

When he got out of the cab, I caught sight of an unfortunately placed hole in the backside of his old sweatpants. I hobbled close behind him as camouflage.

Inside were the sounds and smells of the day: football, ice in glasses, the cacophony of a family gathering its wits for the big production number. My hostess noticed the hole in his pants and offered the cabdriver the most comfortable chair in the house and then a seat at the table and, later, one on the couch to watch the Giants. What I saw were all the old friends from my community who kept streaming in to say something to the nice cabdriver who had brought me home for the holidays. And who had stayed for dinner.

That night on the ride back, I sat in the front seat, and for the first time Manhattan looked like a candelabra'd banquet laid out from the Bronx to the Battery. The meter was off. In fact, the cabbie said that the fare for the trip out was canceled. He helped me out of the cab and up my stairs. I didn't give him my phone number; he didn't ask.

Two weeks later, I was still laid up. Around dinnertime my buzzer rang. It was one of New York's finest cabdrivers delivering a hot meal for me. Nothing more, but, more to the point, nothing less.

What about less emotionally charged holidays? They, too, make great jumping-off points for your consideration. Countless online calendars and almanacs list dates and their significance. I use them freely. After locating a date—America's Labor Day, for instance—ask yourself how to make it uniquely yours. It's there for the mining.

Sifting through my Wal-Mart-sized unconscious, I'd start to think about what it is that people choose to labor over, which will remind me of my obituary addiction, and I'd start taking notes.

My first daily obit fix is online, reading the *New York Times* stories of the famous dead. Two daily newspapers are delivered to my house, and I study the paid death notices, which, incredibly, some newspapers do not run online.

My hope is that mine is a modest addiction. Weekends I go on a bender. We get three Sunday newspapers—my husband, frequently my supplier and always my codependent, is, after all, a newspaper editor—and I recline with them, selecting one obit at a time like a bon bon from a box. As I read each obit, my wonder at what it is that everybody does with their lives melts away.

My all-time favorite obit is that of the composer Robert Merrill, a Tin Pan Alley tunesmith who couldn't read music but who wrote "People," "How Much Is That Doggie in the Window," "Mambo Italiano," "Love Makes the World Go Round," and hundreds of other songs, all of which he composed on a five-and-dime xylophone. After his songs earned him more than $250,000, he bought a more expensive xylophone. It cost $6.98. His one rule was that every tune he wrote had to be hummable.

All that in one obit: Just keep things hummable. What an admirable ethic. After reading that, I swiped my three-year-old daughter's xylophone and plopped it on my desk so I'd try to do that every day.

They die, and you live and learn. It works for me. And when it's my turn to be read over and clipped (or not), I hope something about my labors will leave somebody inspired. But that's dicey, because we get into all kinds of trouble when we try to be admired.

It's a great stumbling spot for writers: wanting to be admired. Writing something that makes them sound admirable, writers can come off sounding like the worst kind of self-serving schmucks. The best example of this is a parenting column from someone who is always right. I hate those and wonder why anyone would choose to write from the point of view of knowing all the right things to do with children, when the far more interesting (as well as far more true) vantage point is that of fumbling through the day while living under the bruising scrutiny of a three-year-old.

When I was driving with my daughter when she was little, she asked, "Mommy, what do you do?"

"You mean for work?"

"Yes."

"I'm a writer." In the rearview mirror, I saw a puzzled look from the backseat. "I stay home during the day and write stories."

She stared.

"I write books."

Her eyes widened. Oh, how I imagined that would make me her hero.

"Mommy," she said, snapping her arms across her chest, "it's not nice to write in your books."

And after that, she hoarded her crayons, perhaps suspecting that, left at home without a sitter, I was going to scribble in her books. I asked for it. I was looking for admiration and got just what I deserved. I hope to improve before my obit runs.

See what I'm doing here? I'm letting you in on how I might build that personal essay to run on Labor Day, thinking by typing, deciding what might go in and what might not. The hoarding-crayons vignette will not make it into the piece—overkill, as well as too cute—though the memory of it percolates up when I consider the topic of how we labor in our lives. I'll jot it down and use it later, and then get back to thinking about the fruits of one's labors. And as I do, I might think about that twentieth college reunion of mine, where the campus looked like the spoils-of-war scene in *Aida*, and, turning to those reference books on my desk, I'll look up who was riding home with those spoils and find out it was Radames, who had kicked some serious rebel butt and returned triumphant to Egypt with elephants, camels, and every other weight-bearing animal slumping under tons of gold, silver, food, and slaves. Researching him, I'll learn that in Egypt, at least, he was a genuine conquering hero.

I'll think about standing in the shade at my small liberal arts college, watching the caravan of sport utility vehicles groaning under the weight of sailboards, mountain bikes, sea kayaks, and jogging strollers—and at least one set of fertility-assisted triplets—wondering what battles had rendered this massive display of spoils. What had we conquered? Had we written any hummable tunes?

Which would be a good place to go back to my obit addiction, and

I'd say something about the wealth of America making some of us woozy, leaving us to wonder about the value of labor and whose labor is actually valued. When I feel this way, my obit addiction sobers me right up. Right there in black and white—lacking the cars and the sailboards, and whatever else we might simply acquire—the obits simply state the facts of a life, allowing me to run the bases of a person's years and hear the cheering, see those long strides of human endeavor, recognize those great failings and those long last looks of good-bye.

And what will I need here now for this piece to work?

What's called a kicker. A last line, which in an essay could be fairly snappy if you like that kind of thing. That last line doesn't always have to be like the couplet at the end of a Shakespearean sonnet, nicely rounding up all we've learned, but hey, it's not a bad standard for starters.

Hmmm. So maybe if I start the whole piece with something like "My name is Marion, and I am an obit addict," I finish it with the line "So give me a double. And, please, don't offer me a cure."

Use it or lose it

Raise your hand if you tell the same stories over and over: that tale you tell about your twentieth college reunion, the Thanksgiving debacle, the Seder-masochistic tale of woe.

What if I said you could never tell them again unless you first wrote them down, that you'd lose them if you didn't use them?

I think you'd write them down.

But first, be really afraid.

Counterphobia

There are many adages about writing, though one that's particularly helpful is to write what scares you. We're all scared of being wrong. I am, every day, as a parent. And I'm glad, since I've never learned anything by being right.

Big stuff scares us. I'm the most squeamish person I know, as well as a fainter, always choosing the most public of places to go down, including once, in the toothpaste aisle of my local supermarket. Merely thinking of standing still makes me sweat; there were chairs at the head of the church at our wedding ceremony. Sure that I'd faint during the rites, I would not have made it down the aisle without seeing them there. My behavior at the sight of blood is idiotic, so going to my first autopsy presented real issues until I discovered that surprising things can happen when you write from a place of fear.

I went to my first autopsy, and here is what I learned: Human ribs can be clipped with the shears I use to prune my floribunda roses. The smell of a man dead for more than one week is far more fearsome than his look. Dust casting from the round blade of a saw uncapping a skull will empty a room of prosecutors. While a body may or may not have been someone's temple, there is something divine inside it.

I figured I would hate an autopsy. As someone who has never watched her own blood drawn and has to lie down for the procedure, chances were good that I would, at least, faint.

But I was writing a book about forensic science, so I had to enter the morgue. Yet I did so with clenched fists and teeth. The room was lined with clear jars of body parts awaiting their day in court. The stainless-steel table was at the center. A scale hung over its foot, and above was a tray cradling utensils that looked more like hardware than surgical supplies.

One wall was dissected by the stainless-steel doors of the coolers. Everything got real quiet when one was unlocked. The diener slid out the body bag, then pushed it over to the autopsy table, and shifted the body onto it. In German, the word "diener" has meanings that include "attendant," "responsible manservant," and "slave." In the course of their day, American dieners will cut, saw, clean, and sew. But first, they unzip the bag.

Right then was when I ran out of fear. There was just no more left. It had never happened before.

At some point during a recent holiday, between the time I was peeling vegetables and ironing linen napkins, somewhere in North America a man was strangled in his own home. The hyoid bone in his neck was fractured. During the autopsy, it was filleted out of his throat and laid out on a sheet to reveal three distinct notches where it had been snapped like a kitchen match.

By the time the forensic pathologist dissected out the fatal point of contact, we had been in the room most of a day, and in that time I had left the only chair in the room and edged closer to the story, the body, looking deeper into the corpse of someone who had been volunteering his time, befriending the needy, and buying a new car only the week before.

It may have taken only seconds for my fear to drain out and be replaced with something else. And in that small moment there was—maybe in those small moments there always is—a choice. For me, it was to flee the room or to shove the fear aside and fill the space with something better.

The forensic pathologist who performed the autopsy is someone I know. We've had long talks about the effects of this work on the people who do it. He has told me that he thinks he may now be an atheist. I can relate to that. I'm well aware that I go to God only when I am in need. This forensic scientist has been more candid than others I've interviewed. He questions a God who could allow people to do what he sees them do to one another. And I've understood him, completely, each time he's said it.

But standing over the wide-open body of a murdered man, I wasn't so sure.

What I felt was pure, unabashed wonder at the way things work in the body of humankind. Just the way the ribs lunge out to harbor the heart and lungs, that alone was more compelling than squeamishness or the fear of the karma emanating from a murdered man.

My Catholic friends speak of near occasions to sin when they have a brush with something unsavory. For me, this was a near occasion to faith, perhaps a glimpse while I stood there looking. Just a flash.

Just enough to get me out of the chair and maybe nothing more. But God knows, faith has been built on less.

LIBELING THE DEAD, AND OTHER FEARS

Being afraid in the autopsy suite helped me write the first essay I read on NPR. Entitled "My First Autopsy," it's the section you just read, beginning three paragraphs after that previous subhead, "Counterphobia." It starts with "I went to my first autopsy..." and ends with the line that begins "But God knows..."

The day after the autopsy, while transcribing my notes, thinking they would be used solely for the book I was contracted to write, I discovered the material for that essay. Though I wore a wintergreen-oiled surgical mask in the cooler, my senses were actually heightened to the point where I was scribbling about faith and fear; I had seen and felt more there than on any other reporting experience—and it was alive in the notebook, the language itself heightened in the scribbling.

Fear is with us all the time. Afraid of making bad parenting mistakes, scared of blurting out the single thing that might damage my marriage, fear of what might be said every time the topic of our mother comes up with my sister and me—all of those make really good subjects. We're all afraid at the margins of our main roles, which makes it a great place to write from.

And while a fear of death is a good topic, as are the dead themselves, many students in my classes confess their fear of writing about dead relatives, afraid of the response they might get from the living. There are so many better reasons not to write; each of us possesses an endless stream of them, though perhaps the most word-stopping one I hear is what the family—whether living or dead—might think.

Write the piece—revisions, edits, the whole shebang—and then let's see what we have. Worrying what someone will say before you even write it makes about as much sense as shopping now for what you'll wear on the *Today* show. Write it. And if we must, later we'll take the family pulse. And then we'll shop.

Who knows—the person you're writing about may have died by the time you're done, leaving you free and clear to publish your tale, since legally you can't libel the dead. Still alive? Okay, too, since the truth is the best defense, and you are telling the truth, your version of it, chanting the soothing phrase "This is the way I remember it" or "The way it seemed to me" or "In my version of the tale," and writing on.

May I? Yes, you may.

When choosing a topic, ask yourself the simple question "Can I write about this?" Not "may I," since you may do any damn thing you like.

Can I? If so, great.

If not, that's fine, too. Maybe you're living with something right now that's too difficult to write in real time. So take notes; during a long writing life, you will find another time and, more to the point, another angle from which to view anything.

This is true even when the events you choose to portray become as serious as family damage. Even the most polite, best-intentioned families can do very clever damage. And that makes good copy, as does the tragic damage done when people collide, though writing gets trickier faster for victims of abuse who choose to tell their tales.

Over the years, my class has heard of every kind of abuse. And every time an abuse memoir is read, I remind the students before we critique it to stick to what's on the page, not to judge the actions, offer therapeutic help, or their own tales of woe; not to ask what happened next, if it's not on the page. It's a necessary prescription if we're to do the work.

First I look for what works with the piece. Memoirs about abuse will be cluttered in whorled images, voices, and meaning, but there will be a uniquely illuminating sentence in paragraph eight, or a reverberating image in paragraph twelve, and we'll start there, since drawing the writer's attention to what works is the very best way to get more of the same.

Perhaps what works is the point of view of the child who experienced the abuse. What happens if you transpose your tale to another age? Can you tell it, as did one student, as your eight-year-old self? She had us watch as her father found her crammed into a corner of the attic, and she recounted what she told herself, how she demanded of herself not merely that she survive but to thrive, how she clung to the images of school and freedom and friends, so that years later, as a well adult, she was sitting in our class, teaching us about the topic of abuse.

Transporting yourself back to a younger you, remember to use the vocabulary of your eight-year-old self, and include nothing from popular culture after that time—no movie references or books, no cognitive awareness of a teenager. Remaining in the worldview of the eight-year-old, you might finally tackle something tricky you pine to explore.

Or you may simply wait until you have something new to say.

Years after the magazine pieces and the book on our family's struggle with Alzheimer's disease, I scribbled down this sentence: *More than twenty years ago, my mother's mind went to battle with something and lost.*

It's a good opening line. But where to go from there? The topic has changed for me over the years. But how?

How you once felt about something may bear little resemblance to how you feel about it after twenty years, or three months, or merely after a minute of careful consideration, when you discover that instead of merely importing responses from your family, you indeed have views that are wholly different from theirs. This can be a good essay topic, especially if yours is a redneck family and you became a blue-stater, or, like one of my students, your two lesbian mothers ran a bar and a head shop during your formative years, and you've grown up to be a suburban woman with a minivan, a husband, and three kids. Both of these writers are voices of authority on family influence and how things change.

"More than twenty years ago, my mother's mind went to battle with something and lost." At first, the sentence seemed to be about what had been taken from us, but when I scrawled it, it was harvest season. I was involved in a project on how to restore the right to worship to those from whom it had been taken away. I had been deeply disturbed to witness Alzheimer's patients, and others who can be disruptive, turned away from their places of worship.

Hard as I tried, I could not follow that sentence about my mother with another accounting of loss, particularly when all around me lay the bounty of autumn and in my head was this project on faith. Suddenly it seemed a good time to take stock.

In my memories of my mother, I always seem to be playing the role of the audience, there in the good seats. Even when I think of her now, my heart sits right down in the same place, paying the same sort of attention it always has.

My mother's name was Allene. She was a descendant of Ethan Allen, the Revolutionary War hero, and her parents gave her their own form of the family name. As a child, she was a tomboy. In college, she studied journalism and went on to become the society editor of the *Long Island Star Journal*, a New York daily newspaper that folded in the 1950s. She became a wife and mother, a Girl Scout leader, a visiting nurse volunteer, and a teacher—each experience adding to the bounty of her life. And then she got Alzheimer's.

Within five years, she could no longer speak or recognize my sister or me. And while we still did things together, she was always agitated and seemed uninterested in anything but watching television and smoking.

Except on Sundays, when we went to church. There, she was calm. On the last day before she went into a nursing home, I took her to church as usual.

Exhausted and leaning my head against the side of the pew, I noticed that my mother was singing all the hymns. Then she said all the words of the Lord's Prayer. This from a woman who could no longer speak my name.

Years later, the project took my mind back to those moments of refuge. Without meaning to, we bar patients from places of worship at the moment they and their family members need it most. When someone cannot sit still or be quiet or remain continent, we discourage their presence in our churches and synagogues. We don't want them to disrupt the ceremony and the spiritual solitude.

One autumn, a bunch of us in Troy, New York, put together a harvest-themed service for people like my mother, wanting to celebrate what we had as opposed to focusing on what we had lost to Alzheimer's. Our group included a rabbi, an Episcopal priest, and a Presbyterian minister. The service intermingled the themes of Sukkoth from the Jewish tradition with Christianity's harvest hymns and prayers. We invited patients and their caregivers. I wrote a prayer for the caregivers and one for the patients. We convinced the priest to keep his sermon under five minutes, we used a lot of music, and we encouraged walking around throughout the service.

When it came to the traditional offertory, we passed around baskets of apples; instead of collecting money, we hoped to give something to the patients and their families.

Going from patient to patient, I carried a huge African basket filled with apples. One very ill woman was curled up in a wheelchair, her head slumped on her chest, her hands tightened into the gnarls we associate with the very last days of life. Her caregiver shook her head, indicating that the woman would not be able to hear or understand me. But I wanted the old woman to have an apple. I got down on my knees and tried to make eye contact. It was impossible. I tried to open one of her hands, but it was like a knot. Giving up, I stood to walk to the next patient.

At that moment, the offertory hymn began. The organ began the opening bars of "How Great Thou Art," and my husband, an accomplished baritone, began to sing what we had expected to be a solo.

The woman uncurled. She straightened up in her wheelchair. At the top of her lungs, she sang every word.

The caregiver gasped. I literally staggered back, then watched as the joy and triumph of this woman revealed itself. She sang from someplace that most of us thought was long gone. As the song ended, she curled back into her chair. But we had reached her.

There, amid the losses that had been diagnosed and charted, amid the grief of a family at what had looked like the end of life, was this offering of hope, this small bounty, this plenty, this harvest tale.

AND THEN THERE'S LOOKING AT IT THIS WAY

Only a few days after that service, my mother died. We lived with that damn disease for fifteen years, but her death still wrenched me into a dumb state of ignorant grief. Then, at Christmas, something happened, though at the time, lacking any sense of wonder, I merely made a few notes on the event, hoping to use them later.

Several years went by before I began to realize that every time the holidays come around, I am reminded that I really should do something with my mother's ashes. And I will, though now, more than twenty years since she died, this length of time out of the grave, or water or air, is no longer all that startling. My father's ashes have been in a closet at my sister's house for more than thirty years, and though I tell myself that the right ritual will present itself, even the turn of the century came and went without inspiring an interment.

Since our mother was so young when she showed the first signs of Alzheimer's disease, she was of great medical interest, carefully monitored in life and autopsied at death. The autopsy was prearranged by the medical facility where she'd been tracked, as was the transfer of the body to a crematorium in Manhattan, about three hours from where I live. I think the name of the place was Sal's.

My mother died the day after Thanksgiving. Despite the holiday, I called the crematorium and was put right through to Sal, the owner, who said all the right things: He was sorry for my loss, there was no reason to attend the cremation, and he took checks.

He said he'd send them after the check cleared.

"Send what?" I asked.

"The remains."

"Send them?"

"In the mail," he said.

FedEx, it seems, does not take human remains.

Ten days later, my check bounced.

For whatever the subliminal and not-so-subliminal reasons a woman might have for bouncing a check at Sal's Lower East Side Crematorium, it did—or rather, I should say, I did bounce it. And while I'd like to say that my bookkeeping got undone in the planning of a funeral and burial, we know that's not true.

I overnighted a money order and apologized profusely to Sal on the phone and in writing. Ten days later I said I was sorry again, over the phone, when the ashes still hadn't shown up. And in another two weeks' time, when still the package hadn't come.

Then, on Christmas Eve, the phone rang. It was the nice lady at my pint-size rural post office.

"I have a package for you," she said cheerily.

It wasn't surprising, considering the season. But I knew better. "I'll be right down," I said.

The postmistress was wearing a Santa hat.

That helped. There in her hands was a brown paper package that easily could have contained a large can of coffee.

"It's heavy," she said, smiling.

She and I saw each other nearly every day, but she didn't know about the death. My mother's life had been over years earlier, but only my friends knew she had finally died.

So the postmistress stood there in her hat, displaying her best holiday cheer, a plate of cookies at her elbow, behind a counter cross-gartered with ribbon like a big wrapped gift. I started to sweat right about the time she put the package to her ear and started to shake it.

"I hope it's not broken," she said as the contents shifted back and forth.

"Let's see who it's from," I said, an octave higher than my usual speaking voice as I gently lowered it from her ear to the counter.

Sal had been good enough to use his first and last name, and not that of his business. That was a gift.

"Ooh," she said, "someone in New York City. You know him?"

I eased the package from her hands into mine, and then, when it was securely against my heart, I was able to feel how to make the panic stop and allow the private cleanup work of grief to begin.

"It's from Uncle Sal," I said. "On my mother's side."

Does my mother live in New York City, too?

"No," I said, not looking at the box between us. "She died some time ago."

"I'm sorry," she said. "What do you think it is?" she asked, beaming back at the box.

"Same thing he always sends," I said. "Bulbs." I gave the box a tender shake. "Packed in sand. Lovely flowers you start indoors in winter." And I backed away from the counter, cradling the box in my arms. "Happy holidays," I said.

Get ready to drive

Sometimes you have to let the big story climb into the backseat, allowing it to give only small directions without driving the tale.

One topic, two essays, one book, several cowritten books, a few others for which I wrote the introductions, one *New York Times* "Science Times" piece, a *Discover* magazine piece, a *New York Times Magazine* piece—these are a few of the stories I've published with my mother's illness at the center, off to the side, sometimes in the background, depending on what the piece was about or on how I chose to wrap it each time. One piece of information—my ill mother—used many ways.

Things like Alzheimer's happen—they're what we call life. What you do with them is writing. And while all of those experiences I chronicled are true, not one of them is the whole truth. Going for the whole truth is a fool's errand, and while many writers chase it unsuccessfully all their lives, they'd publish more, as well as understand more about life, if they took on life one theme at a time. Doing that requires disciplining your subconscious, asking it to look for what you need, on topic, on demand.

And after that, we rip off the tourniquet and we write.

Chapter 3

Having Sex with Roger

A POSTCARD DATED April 11, 1989, sits above my desk, and it has ever since I received it from my friend Annie—confidante, maid of honor, pal of thirty years. On it is pasted a clipping, a few lines from some unnamed magazine.

It reads:

> ### *Today's Tip for Fiction Writers:*
>
> A good way to "liven up" the plot of a novel is to give the characters some romantic interest.
>
> WRONG: Doreen entered the room.
>
> RIGHT: Doreen entered the room and had sex with Roger.

One of my favorite possessions, the note (and its thinking) is a lovely parody of the bad advice writers can get, as well as a great reminder of how much fun it can be to write about sex.

While I ban raw pornography in my class, we do love a good sex essay, though "sex," you now know, of course, is too big a topic and must be broken down to its integral parts like, say, the penis.

Anyone who raises kids knows that the penis is a great topic. So many parenting column inches are dedicated each year to this one subject and how to talk about it, or avoid talking about it, that all parents must have a penis story or two up our sleeves. And as I mentioned earlier, the beauty is that you can write about penises without completely understanding them, making the penis another of the greater things to write about.

I learned this lesson when my daughter was five and she told me she wanted to be a boy. More precisely, she said she wanted a penis.

I thought I'd be good at this. As happens with most breathtaking parent-child exchanges, we were driving. The gaping silence from backseat to front was suddenly filled by my child listing the names of seemingly blessed boys, ticking them off on her little fingers as my mind raced with what exactly to say.

"Ben has a penis," she said. "And Alex has one and Brian."

Once home, I bought some time, suggesting we hold our discussion inside the house. Coats off and hung up, I was on.

My daughter stood looking into my face, and I began, embracing my big chance to imprint informed sexuality on my little girl. The best place to start would be with a map of the human body. En route to the bookshelf, I launched into an ambitious preamble on how the sexes differ and how everyone needs to be tolerant of that. I then teetered around the penis, amusing myself along the way with my judicious omission of any easy shots at its obvious pros and cons.

My hand was actually on my copy of *Our Bodies, Ourselves*, and I was on a regular roll when I noticed that my child had her hand on her hip and was shifting her weight from side to side, looking a little bored.

"Where was I?" I asked.

"The penis."

Time for some maternal sincerity. "Why do you want one, dear?" I asked, crouching down in that earnest way mothers without a clue often do.

"Because the toilet seat is so cold," she said, and there you have it: another use for the penis, as an essay illustration of a larger theme.

What is this piece about? Humility, as illustrated daily when parenting. Parents would be much better off if, like defense attorneys, we knew the answer to the question before we asked it. Except we never do, which makes a very nice place to write from.

RIPPED FROM THE HEADLINES

Memoirists can obviously write about themselves—motivated by things (like the penis) that they have on them at all times. But what about the headlines? The news is motivating; things happen, and we should react.

I can get pretty worked up reading the news, particularly when we seem to be ignorant and shouldn't be, which is how I felt during the international genome-mapping backslapping period, when few of my friends knew what the genome was. It's kind of like taking someone from Minsk to a Mets game and neatly defining the infield fly rule while neglecting to define "base."

How to explain the genome? I wondered, which got me thinking about inheritance and the obvious aspects of me that I've seen before, like my father's red hair and his knees. Thinking in propinquities reminded me of my other inheritances, including my collection of recipe boxes from dead relatives.

These boxes are as much a lineage as my dad's looks. And they link my family's ancestral nourishment from South Dakota to Indiana and back to England, Scotland, and Germany. They reveal who I am, lacking, as they do, any recipes from Africa or from Asia—that is, unless you consider my mother-in-law's Spam chop suey to be in any way Eastern, which would be seriously stretching this recipe. Its four basic ingredients are Spam, fat, rice, and a can of cream-of-mushroom soup. Each recipe in Lillian's box, in fact, includes some combination of these four.

If you consider their ingredients alone, you can see each of the recipes in each of the boxes I've collected as a steady diet for nourishment, disease, or some uneven prandial existence in between. They are also a handy way to explain genetics.

Here's what I mean. Let's say that the genome is my mother-in-law's recipe box. If there are twenty-three little colored tabs sticking up within it—beef, poultry, cheese, casseroles, hors d'oeuvres, and so on—they are the twenty-three chromosomes in the human body. Within each of these are genes—or, in this case, the recipes, including, of course, the chop suey with its four basic ingredients. The human genome equivalent of these ingredients are adenine, cytosine, guanine, and thymine, written in genetic transcription as A, C, G, and T, and just like Lillian's four staple ingredients, these four are always present in every gene.

The idea of recipe exchange as an explanation for genetics also extends to the frequent e-mails sent to my dear friend Elizabeth. Both of us inherited an uneasy sense of dinnertime being catch-as-catch-can. We both hoped to not pass this on to our daughters. Back and forth between us travels a fluent battery of recipes cadged off the Internet. Ready to go with the touch of a file-attachment button, these recipes are simply cloned.

By contrast, my mother-in-law's recipes are written by hand, transcribed over and over for her children and friends and therefore prone to typos and changes but always having the same basic ingredients. This process is pretty much what goes on in replication, where the gene is copied and passed along. I have the box she made for her youngest child, my husband, in which she adapted the chop suey recipe to a serving for one; in her large-box version, it's adapted for twenty.

When we married, my husband brought his mother's recipe boxes into our home and I brought mine. For holidays, we undergo genetic recombination, uniting our two families' inherited recipes and laying them out as a single feast before our unsuspecting child, who will grow up thinking that this is the food—including the Spam chop suey—of her ancestors. Which is particularly piquant, since she was adopted in China.

HOW WE WRITE ABOUT WHAT WE CHOOSE TO TELL

The penis and the Spam chop suey stories run the topic gamut from literally what we have right under our noses to what's out in the wide world. They remind you that anything and everything is yours for the mining.

So let's mine.

Choose that story you've been itching to write. Perhaps the stories I've told you here have provoked a memory or a scene. Get out one of those index cards you've been carrying around. Get a pen. And get the calendar. What is today's date? Now look one week into the future. That's your deadline. Note that date in the upper right-hand corner of the index card.

Whether you are choosing to write a blog post, an essay, or a book, you must write them one scene at a time. So, use that algorithm and, if you need to, noodle around for a while until you know what that scene is about. When you know, write that theme on the front of the card. On the back of the index card, write down the pertinent details that illustrate that theme, from fragments of dialogue to colors, smells, and shapes you can recall. If this piece is a single essay, tape that index card right to your computer screen, with the front side out, to remind you what it's about. When writing a book, this method works as well, giving each scene its own card and attaching them to your computer screen as you write. At other times these cards should be tacked on a corkboard in chronological order, to be added to as you recall more details.

In the course of writing a number of essays, I might choose to embrace my most private fears in one piece and then keep you at an emotional arm's length in another, and even with that shift of intimacy, it's possible that all of those essays—whether they were originally written for my family, my blog, for public radio, or as pieces for other books—might have some connection to one another. Placed together and bolstered by more pieces, these seemingly disparate tales told on myself might meld into a book, as they did for this book you are now reading. What they would need, though, is a structure.

STRUCTURE. PERIOD.

"Structure" is the dreaded word for those of us who regularly submit book proposals. Immediately after I pitch an idea, my agent or editor will ask, "What's the structure?" as in, "How are you going to do it?"

Will your memoir be 235 pages, twelve chapters, tied together by three themes called Book(s) One, Two, and Three? What will the three books have in common? What's really being asked is how you plan to dole out your argument. What sustainable grid will you use to lay out that argument, one fact at a time, so that we understand it, and perhaps even agree with you at the end? Even if you are writing your memoirs for the very best of reasons—to give them to your children—mere chronology is not a structure and is never the best way to go. Instead, consider structuring the book to answer the question of how you grew up to be who you are—a naturalist, married to your spouse, a doctor, a skeptic—rather than merely plodding along a decade at a time; that is, if you want someone to read it, and you do.

"What's your structure?" has probably sent more memoir writers home to drink gin straight out of the bottle than any other question in the unsteady history of publishing. Because it all seems like such a good idea to write of your family's immoderate behavior, your son's illness, your marriage, your child's suicide, or your recovery…until someone actually asks you how you're going to do it.

But that's what they want to know: How are you going to do it? Because if you can communicate that, and your writing sample is good, publishers have some assurance that the money they're thinking of handing you will actually produce a book and not merely a long hot bender in Guam.

In Elizabeth Gilbert's best-selling memoir, *Eat, Pray, Love*, the author chronicles the year she shed her belongings and attachments and went on a journey of discovery, choosing places she could explore pleasure (eat), spirituality (pray), and, of course, love. She chose to tell the tale in 108 short chapters, the number of prayer beads on the japa mala, a Buddhist prayer-bead string. This is her structure.

Even short pieces have structure. You've noticed the ones that don't. If reading them felt like trying to hold pudding instead of, say, a sandwich, they lacked structure. When the contents ooze out in all directions at once, with no recognizable shape, the thing would benefit from some structure.

Structure is not to be confused with an outline, or the order in which you will tell things. Say you want your structure to be the Ws of life—who, what, when, where, and why (which, by the way, would work as a structure). You divide your book into five chapter titles in which you cover those topics. Maybe you want your structure to resemble your house, with each chapter as a room, reflecting a logical progression from basement to attic. Such elaborate construction is best left to long-form memoir, though reading online it's clear that most blogs lack structure, their topics seeping off in every direction at once.

In long-form memoir, the only way to find a structure is to first reduce your book idea to one sentence.

Okay. I see what you're doing. You're about to put this down. Don't. Do this now or you'll fall into the abyss of never writing the book and instead merely talking about it for years. More divorces can be tied to unwritten books than any other undone task I can think of. Don't bore your relatives. Enthrall us.

So let's do this now together. Let's write your sentence.

Let's say your one sentence—your argument (and all books are an argument, no matter how small)—is that life is really hard unless you get a good cat to live with. Great. Here's how that will break down. By each phrase: Life. Is hard. Really hard. Unless. You get. A good cat. To live with.

Well, there are your seven chapters. Don't believe me?

Life: Who you are. *Is hard. Really hard*: First show us hard, then show us really hard. One chapter each. *Unless*: This is where you show us that you are open to alternatives. *You get*: This is where you show us all the things you've tried in order to make your life better, like speed dating, dieting, drinking heavily, perhaps. *A good cat*: Maybe you've had bad cats or good cats. Tell us. *To live with*: Show us living with that one good cat. Maybe there is a sad ending. Or a happy one. Or a sad one turned happy when the good cat dies and you have the courage to try again with a new cat. See how this works?

But it absolutely depends on the one sentence. It's the spine upon which you build the rest of the body.

In shorter pieces, the tried-and-true template for foolproof structure is the bagel, and it remains the best, simplest, and most dependable way to get an essay opened and shut. Just make a simple circle, beginning with one image—your current parakeet's remarkable intelligence as evidenced by one feat—and go back and reference that intelligent act at the end. Open and close with the same idea, put some proof in the middle, the ring is complete, and you're done. As you improve, lop off one of the references to that idea, knowing that you've so securely stitched both your theme and proof of that theme into your piece that you no longer need the entire bagel. Try the simple method first, using it for both essays as well as for longer pieces, and you'll get something on the page, though I warn you, it won't be pretty.

THE VOMIT DRAFT

Gary, my best friend and hands-down favorite science writer, calls the first pass the vomit draft—and for good reason, since there is no such thing as a good first draft. In her marvelous book *Bird by Bird*, Anne Lamott calls it the "shitty first draft," and I love that, but Gary's term reminds us that real creativity includes both physical pain as well as a soundtrack. Retching and moaning. Writing may require both. If it didn't, every brain surgeon could do it.

The biggest shock of writing is that it's difficult. Why? As St. Teresa of Avila famously said, it's because "more tears are shed over answered prayers than unanswered ones." Done with purpose, writing is hard work. When you practiced with prompts, something always flowed, though all of it remains in some notebook. Much like playing tennis with a pro who hits every shot right to you, those exercises convinced you that you had this writing thing nailed. When you're alone in a room trying to write with intent, it's mind-slammingly hard. Though not impossible.

And right after my students experience the difficulty, perhaps the next most shocking piece of information they receive is that NPR saw draft number forty-five of my Spam chop suey essay. And then I tell them that it was the third total rewrite of my last book that got the check from my publisher. And always they dismiss it; I now recognize a default look on the faces, that precise gauzy gaze when, instead of listening, they revert to planning their *Today* show wardrobe, thinking that this rewrite/edit thing happens to everyone *but them*.

Enjoy the thought. And then have a look at that vomit draft of yours.

And please don't tell me your husband liked it. Of course your wife liked it. Do you think that someone who depends on you for food, sex, and shelter is going to say something else to you? That they liked it means nothing. It's a mess, it's supposed to be a mess, and if it's not a mess, then you don't yet have what you need, so chuck up another one and let's see what we've got.

It's called the vomit draft, too, because it will both stink and be pretty much everything you've got inside you. In there is beauty and success and everything you ever dreamed of. So learn to love a vomit draft like it's your new best gal.

What did the vomit draft of the Spam chop suey story look like? Originally begun as a simple transcription of recipes from my mother-in-law's metal box, it was typed up after one-too-many dinner-party-tellings when my husband coolly suggested I write it down, that maybe there was something "to" this story. That's code in our house for "use it or lose it," that the story is getting tired.

In the next draft appeared a mere mention of Lillian's recipe box, a slight reference to all the dead women whose recipe boxes I own. As the women took over the tale, there was Janet, my mother's best friend, and the story of her late-in-life, though exemplary, marriage, and the piece became a recipe for happiness until my husband's sister appeared on the page, as did the infant she left behind when she died. About ten days into writing a dirge about women and calories and tears, I put it away, having nearly mauled the thing beyond recognition.

Weeks later, while I was puttering in the kitchen, the radio doled out yet another piece of data from the genome, and a structure for the essay descended, a kind of grid appearing in my tired head. I realized that by caging this unruly recipe tale within the bars of this genome story, I'd have an answer to my question: "What the hell is this piece on recipe boxes about?"

That four main ingredients make up both a gene and nearly everything my mother-in-law cooked startled even me, and I actually ran to my office. Frightened by the fragile connection, I needed to wire them together before the thing fell apart.

Two, three days and twenty or twenty-five drafts later, the thing had heft. At Draft 45, it went to NPR (eliciting an incredulous call from a science editor). Two years later, a repurposed version was an integral device in a book I wrote titled *The Roots of Desire*, which recounts the history of red hair.

Gypsies, tramps, and thieves

I hate that Cher song, but why should I suffer alone when we can now both have it in our heads until Tuesday? It is what floods my brain each time I say in class, "Maxims, stats, clichés." That's precisely what you need to use to pave your draft—all that crazy crap in your head, including maxims, proverbs, clichés, tired old phrases, misspellings, bumper-sticker aphorisms, Cher lyrics, treacly bywords, needlepoint-pillow prophecies, dictum/dicta, and whatever else you've got. Write it down. It's all going to go away later, but these old familiars are place markers until your argument takes shape and the right language falls into place.

It may sound counterintuitive to urge you to get even Cher on the page, so take this as the well-picked scab of a reformed perfectionist. The other method, where you choose each word carefully as you go? It's the death of writing. I would argue that in no other form of writing is the use of saccharine, vomity, clichéd place markers more appreciated than in memoir, since they are the fastest route to demystifying your own experiences, allowing you to see those experiences for what they are. Attach a couple of tired old phrases to your first bad boyfriend and presto-chango, he becomes an archetype, or better yet, a stereotype, and you'll be freed up to write his badness down to the last chewed toothpick.

Later, we'll edit. Later, we'll throw around French phrases like Flaubert's *le mot juste* (the right word) and light cigars and feel terribly smug, but there's no right word when there's nothing on the page, and right now we need a vomit draft to muck around in. We're not bowling for height and distance here; we're just trying to roll the ball down the lane once, going successfully from wrist to pins. Soup to nuts. See? Just one bad cliché after another; place your bets, fill your dance card, dance with the girl what brung ya, and override the churlish nuns, naysaying cousins, and jealous brain surgeons who think otherwise. This is what real writing is, and it begins with a big, good vomit.

KEEP ON KEEPING ON

When did I write these subheads, like the one above? Late afternoon, ready to knock off, I typed a subhead for the next day's work. It worked for Ernest Hemingway, who reportedly at each day's end wrote the line that would begin the next writing session. It works for me. Try it yourself. This simple device might even generate words that will live in your final draft. Or, like those slivers of wax paper between the slices of the impossible-looking spinning cakes in diners, you can take them out right before you serve up the piece and—voilà!—what a confection.

A vomit draft even for something as small as a blog post could take several tries. A first draft for a personal essay will take a few days; longer forms take longer, and writing out the specific markers you want to hit can be a great help. You can even type up several of those subheads in a row, later filling the copy in between. Think of those subheads or next lines—all done in the name of hospitality, remember?—as welcome mats when you show up the next day. Chances improve that you will show up the next day if there is anything other than a blank screen to greet you.

After a good vomit draft, you'll begin to think you've run out of material, so do some research: Call your sister, open the phone book, visit your local historical society, look at that photo album, use online resources; in all, do some reporting. That's what memoir reporting looks like and may include conducting family interviews or doing institutional research. Visiting my local historical society, I discovered that my house was once a speakeasy. That's waiting to be written about, perhaps commemorating the repeal of the Volstead Act (December 5, 1933), a date I looked up and wrote down. On the next big anniversary, a radio essay might do, but only after it's clear what it's about.

See how this works?

She said what?

The French (of course) have a phrase for it, those bons mots we wish had popped out of our mouths but didn't. *Esprit d'escalier* means "the wit of the staircase," and it's among memoir's most dangerous temptations. Do not go up those stairs.

The desire to have a snappy comeback—to portray ourselves as witty, clever, and informed—is universal. But rarely are we witty on demand. We all wish we'd said some clever thing when we got dumped. We didn't, not out loud and at the time, and when writing memoir we're not allowed to make ourselves sound more snappy than we are.

At moments of confrontation, our inability to spit out what we long to say reveals our frustration; as we walk away, the words that roll in our heads represent our fears, our manners—ourselves—better than any snappy retort. Not being witty when we want to be is far more human than having some patterned repartee. And far more interesting. In fiction and movies, everyone is witty. In nonfiction, we wrestle with the obvious, and we share our humanity. These little moments, revelatory real events, are what turn and shape our lives. So write about those. What do you wish you had said? That might be interesting; it's certainly universal.

But since we rarely carry a notebook when we're getting thrown out by the man we love, how do we resolve the dialogue issue? How can you be accurate?

Instead of replicating events, think about intent. If I don't know exactly how something was actually said, I tell you that a conversation went "something like this," but never alter the intent of the exchange. If there is a moral responsibility in writing nonfiction, it favors the intent of life's actual circumstances.

Here's an example of how people do not talk.

"Hi, Michael. It is so very good to see you, especially since I have not seen you even once, not once, since we went to college at Dartmouth in 1977, graduating in 1981, well, except for that little stint you did in rehab, but then we all took drugs, didn't we, even me, though I'm really wrestling with how to talk to my kids about that, so you really graduated in, what, '91?"

We don't talk like that unless we're off our meds, though beginning writers write that kind of dialogue. It's not only false reporting, but also awkward—revelatory of limited skills and a total misunderstanding of what dialogue can do.

Dialogue is not supposed to move too much information too fast; when it does, it buckles under the weight of the assignment.

How much of this information do we need?

That depends on what the story is about. Reunion, maybe? What dialogue is needed to get us into the scene? Not much more than a quote characterizing the nervous joy at being reunited. Keep it spare, no matter how big the topic. Try not to overexplain: "...I said nervously because we were just reunited after thirty-five years." Instead, show your nervous joy by whipping off your bifocals and shoving them into your bra—if that's what you did. If you did not, you did something else that communicated nervous joy, and you remember it, because now you're a writer, and that's what writers do.

It's the same with observing others. Always on the prowl for something to steal and turn into copy, I'm never above scraping stuff out of others' mouths and regurgitating it into essays. And why not? Truth, as we well know, is much, much more interesting than anything we could ever make up.

You learn this best when parenting, since kids are weird Martians we deprogram and then make into adults. Too bad, since so much is lost in the transformation.

My daughter was four when she first fell in love with a man other than her dad, and this love was someone who would make the heart of any mother just soar: Tall, Jewish, part of a large family, he doted on the needs of my child and encouraged her to eat her vegetables. But there were problems.

We were driving home from school when I first heard about him, when my little girl said that she had a new friend.

"How nice."

"He hangs out by the playground," she told me.

I listened a little more closely.

"He talks to me all day," she said. "Only me."

Now she had my attention. I had read the books. I knew I was not supposed to show her any fear, no matter what the topic. But I also read the news, and I didn't like the sound of this at all.

Tentatively, I asked, "Do you know his name, sweetie?" Her eyes locked onto mine in the rearview mirror.

"Of course," she said. "It's Bibi Geggy."

"Geggy?" I said. "Bibi, you say?" I scribbled it down while still driving.

"He brings his dog," she told me. "It's a really nice dog."

"What's the dog's name?" something made me ask.

"Walter Fleischman," she said, and then she clammed up. Couldn't get another word out of her all the way home.

There were no Geggys in our local phone book and no Fleischmans of any spelling. The next day, her teachers told us that of course no one hangs around the playground and that certainly no one had been talking to our child day after day.

Perhaps another mother would have figured out sooner that he was imaginary. His name should have given him away. Bibi Geggy. What a great name. My child was delighting me, making me laugh. And not from a pratfall or some cutesy kid thing, but from deep within the vast magnitude of her imagination.

Perhaps my daughter originally intended to keep Bibi around for a short while. Maybe he arrived packed-and-ready-to-go after a month or two. But with just the teensiest bit of encouragement from her mother, my daughter's friend stuck around long enough for us to get to know him real well, and I don't regret a minute of it.

Pablo Picasso said he spent his adulthood trying to get back to painting like a child. It's always been one of those quotes thrown into feel-good books and make-art-from-the-science-side-of-your-brain books, but it never meant so much to me as it does when I ponder Bibi and what his extended family brought to mine. There were babies—sometimes five, sometimes ten, depending on the day— whom he cared for with his sister, Acalcia. At some point, Walter Fleischman found honest work as a police dog in Schenectady before finding Mu Shu, his soul mate, and being transferred to a precinct in Queens. Bibi took up with the ever-unsteady Rosie, who wanted to have children, and then he broke it off with her, a decision we all came to agree was best for everyone involved.

And along with his concerns, some of our own family issues were processed through Bibi et al.

For instance, a friend walked out of a bad marriage and came to stay with us. She was in rough shape.

About two days into her visit, my daughter asked me, "What's divorce, Mommy?"

I explained it.

"Well," she said, "Bibi Geggy is divorced."

Didn't know he was ever married.

"Oh, yes. To Acalcia."

"His sister?" I was more than a little alarmed.

"Well, they were married," she explained, almost whispering, "but now they are traveling as brother and sister." And she nodded very knowingly.

The otherwise-intelligent book I once used through my child's development was full of admonitions about providing other outlets for her imagination, not letting her get too dependent on the imaginary friend and not letting him take the heat for any of her bad behavior.

And parenting books are a great topic that all parents are interested in, and they're one way I could have approached an essay, trashing the book I had used that utterly missed the point of our Bibi. He was never held up against her bad behavior. He was always held up to mine. He was patient, made perfect banana-clam cookies, led a daily parade playing the trombone, and never rushed dinner or bath time to get back to work, or so I was told on a fairly regular basis. That means he was a good listener, a creative playmate, and available even on deadline. He still sounds like a much better parent than I am.

And because of that, Bibi and I, well, we got along like peanut butter and jelly. I mean, who doesn't need a role model? I did. Still do. And even though one day Bibi did get packed off with the pacifiers and the Pull-Ups, he continues to remind me—well into adulthood—to appreciate the rewards of thinking like a child. Which also can be a great place to write from.

B-MATTER

Notice what got left out of the Bibi Geggy story.

A few lines up from these words is the exchange where my daughter asks what divorce is, and without dialogue, I say I explained it. At some point in some draft, there was my long definition of divorce, which I killed, because to understand the piece, you need no more characterization of me than what's here. Were this piece about something else, you'd need to know how I feel about divorce. But it's not about that. Deep, deep background, my feelings aren't necessary to the tale.

But what about details that are needed, though not front and center? Known as B-matter, or background matter, your Bs should be well marshaled or you'll tell us either too much or too little.

The best examples of background, and dialogue, are found in screenplays. At my elbow—and available online—are the complete works of Woody Allen, as well as those of the great screenwriter Preston Sturges, who deftly conveys character in gestures, phrases, menu choices, and the lack of galoshes.

Is your sister a Wellesley graduate and fading 1979 New York debutante? That information rests in the solid gold signet ring worn on her pinky, a totemic stamp of Waspy culture that registers as we read. Such cues surround us: baseball hat backward or forward; the red thread of Buddhism around the neck; paper or plastic bags; heels or flats. How about good old Roger? Lingering back there at the beginning of this chapter, awaiting Doreen's entrance and the possibility of sex, is he doing little more than admiring the lovely stiff cuff pleat on his Brooks Brothers shirt? Before she enters the room, does Doreen stop just long enough to slip a ring from her finger?

You tell us.

Chapter 4

The Barbie-Bodied Book

I TOOK TO teaching during recovery. Not from drugs or alcohol, but from a writing course where an exhausted author let twelve eager students eviscerate one another twice a week, all for credit. Nasty as that was, the nastiness wasn't the problem—the real thorn was that the viciousness didn't drive anybody's story forward. Not a single piece got better with rewrite, a phenomenon so unlikely that there had to be a lesson there. Rewrites have to get better. I learned that at the *Times* from the nice guy nobody liked. But that class had a savagery that stopped the work, a meanness I had heard about in one high-profile writing workshop, where the last person standing wins the phone number of the teacher's agent.

Already a published writer, I took the class after leaving Manhattan and moving upstate, where I needed people to talk to about writing. My only class pal was equally amazed that anyone could learn anything this way. We didn't. One thing was clear: If I ever taught writing, gratuitous, nasty comments would be banned. They produce no value in the rewrites. Rewriting makes your original idea better, but for that to happen, first you need to identify what works in the piece.

LEDE ON

There is no such thing as a good first draft. But that vomit draft, that mess you made when you asked yourself to hurl up everything you had collected on one topic, will contain an image or a truth, or a little corner of an idea, a collection of thoughts that will begin to attract your attention, and you must find it there shimmering on the sidelines and learn what to do next.

So, vomit draft in hand, it's on to the real work of writing. Let's again get out that crisp deck of cards from Chapter 1.

You want to start with a fairly dazzling card, something that leads the reader into sentence number two and all the way to the end. In journalism this is called the "lede," dating back to when newspaper type was set in lead. So as not to confuse the two, the crazy spelling was adopted. In this case, your lede is your opener.

My magazine piece on my mother, as well as the book that followed, opened with a phrase that is deliberate and shocking. It was perhaps my 119th lede, blurted out one late night when my magazine editor was set to send me back again for something better. At this point we were three months into working on the piece.

Several nights a week, after our regular shifts at the *Times*, the kind, patient man sat churning my copy as I learned what not to do, and then he asked his simple question: "How did all this start?"

"I thought my mother was going mad when she killed the cats."

And he nodded at me and squinted, taking a kind of stock I didn't quite recognize, turning back to the computer and typing that line. Elton John's glasses, the card in my hand, the beginning of an education, the smack to the head, the gift, that lede instantly clarified what his squint had meant:

If I led with that, there was no backing down. Watching him type those words into that nasty, vomity draft of mine, it was evident just where that piece had to go.

TROUBLE IN THE COSMOS

Of the wretched mistakes I made when first teaching, perhaps my favorite occurred over what is known as the cosmic graph. And because there is a great deal of justice in this world, I got what I deserved.

"What's this?" I asked when critiquing a piece.

"My cosmic graph."

An actual bar graph had been inserted into the copy. Yes, that's right—a bar graph. What I had intended to explain was that right around the fourth paragraph, the writer must tell the reader what the piece is about—what's at stake, what's up in the air, what to value if it's taken away. By that time in an essay (and even sooner in a blog post), readers must know at least that or they get nervous, as one lovely image turns into another, and we panic, wondering how many of these fine details are going to be on the test. Sometimes this cosmic graph is the literary equivalent of a pan shot from the movies, where the camera pulls from the close-up scene of a woman crying at a table, and suddenly you see her in the farmhouse, in the town, in the world, or at least where you need to be for you to understand where we are on the planet. Writing something like "Douglas Manor, in the 1970s, was a place that even John Cheever might find curiously amoral" might do it, or "Love is in fact love when alteration finds" would be fine as well. Sometimes a cosmic graph says something direct like "This is a love story." Perhaps it's "I never thought I'd fall in love," or something slightly obtuse like "Much like faith, perhaps patriotism is a delicatessen plan," or, after several paragraphs describing your mother's progressive decline, "It was Alzheimer's disease."

But in short pieces of memoir, give us a cosmic graph, and we'll have the guide we need to read on.

CHEKHOV'S GUN

In a memoir of any length, the essential guide to what stays in versus what gets cut can be traced at least as far back as one much-referenced gun of Anton Chekhov. Giving writing advice, he wrote to a friend, "One must not put a loaded rifle on the stage if no one is thinking of firing it." Another way I've heard the same sentiment expressed is that if you give a reader a yellow Volkswagen to drive up a hill, you'd damn well better let him drive it down. In other words, every detail needs a reason for being there. Amazing creatures, readers, possessing remarkable memories, they collect each detail like foreign coins but expect to cash in every one of them by the end of the journey.

WE'RE ALL JUST BABES IN THE WOODS

A lifelong friendship was made at the *Times* with one of my bosses, Sydney Schanberg, winner of the Pulitzer for his coverage of Cambodia. Purveyor of jokes such as the "what, in this weather?" anecdote used earlier in this book, he is also the person who gave me the gift of toyland.

A weird abstraction that journalists once used, the full expression is "arrows to toyland," referring to those markers you leave along the way for your reader to follow. Its origin is the operetta *Babes in Toyland* (music by Victor Herbert, libretto by Glen MacDonough), a multitiered confection of nursery rhymes and Christmas imagery, containing some of Herbert's best-known music, including "Toyland" and "March of the Toys."

Even by the time Syd taught it to me, it was said mostly in jest, though I'll resurrect it here, dust it off, and see if we can't make the old thing sing.

Teaching this idea in the first year of my class, had I not been so nervous, even I might have noticed how everyone looked a little round-eyed when I launched into the "arrows to toyland" segment of my two-hour opening-night lecture. Then, a few weeks later, while I was critiquing someone's piece, trying to untangle the essay's gnarly logic, the writer insisted he was only following my instructions and being "Aristotelian." Apparently, the speed at which I speak in my New York accent had transposed "arrows to toyland" into "Aristotelian," and I laughed like hell, threw away my lecture notes, and have never used them again. Now I teach from the work the class brings in, knowing that during our weeks together, every aspect of memoir writing will be raised, including how to lead your readers where you want them to go.

But here (without my accent), perhaps the arrows are helpful, providing a simple device with which to plot your course, by suggesting that you ask yourself what specific bits of information must appear in your story to convince your reader of your argument.

THE BARBIE-BODIED BOOK

Understanding what you're trying to tell us depends on your math. To make this happen, you must plant those markers, or arrows, and lead the reader home. Another way to look at this is that your details must add up. Just as two and two make four, your details, which are nothing more—or less—than subtle illustrations of your argument, must add up to a sum your reader can deduce.

In long-form memoir, by the time that book is done, it had better have one whistle-getting figure, not unlike Barbie's, one that won't let the reader peel his eyes off your argument. The best place to learn this skill is by reading good journalism. And while I use only a few handouts in the class, I can pretty much hand out any old thing I read in the *New York Times*, including a decidedly non-memoir-ish magazine clip I saved from years ago by James Traub. The excerpt is just a paragraph or two of a 5,000-word piece, and I point out but one thing the students should look for—the details.

The *Times* thinks it's a piece about how, "as the United Nations Security Council argued long into the night over the wording of a so-called presidential statement castigating Israel for the bombing attack that killed four U.N. observers in southern Lebanon, Wang Guangya, the Chinese ambassador, blew his stack," according to the Web site abstract.

Early on, Traub tells us that the ambassador smokes, that it has discolored his teeth, and you wonder why you need to know this, but you remember it 5,000 words later, after Traub has deftly woven this tale, making a convincing argument that the world needs to pay more attention to how China defiantly votes with the very countries many of us have trouble supporting. In the last scene, there sits the ambassador, smoking in a lounge with NO SMOKING signs pasted everywhere.

The piece is an example of writing math, and an example of why writers must read widely.

My father used to say that the *New York Times* was a miracle produced every day, and he's right. No matter what platform you choose for reading it, your newspaper will inform you. Like all artists, you need to be informed so that you can react. The more informed you are the better, especially if you want to move from writing merely a personal tale to one that might inform others.

WHEN THE FUR FLIES

Opposite your newspaper's editorial page is a page of columns written by people like you. These are people with points of view, those same people whose voices you hear on both local and national public radio reading the lovely, quirky essays those outlets like to run.

While sometimes we merely want to convince others that life is better with a good cat to love, other times we're just the teensiest bit itching for the fur to fly. In that case, you can write an op-ed.

Of course, not all op-eds are pieces of memoir, but when they are, they employ that invincible weapon of putting a face to an issue. As they say, if you want someone to remember it, either make it rhyme or put it to music. Putting a face to an issue also does that, making it a device that gives an argument its melodic line.

On which of life's big topics have you got some expertise? Are you caregiving an aging relative? Raising children? Have you got a small vignette that illustrates a solution to a large urban problem or one that heightens and adds to our understanding of just how wonderful some overlooked aspect of rural life can be? Perhaps your husband's cancer care gave you a new take on the health care debate. Maybe you teach, and by illustrating how federal budget cuts look in your specific classroom, you can predict how our children may fail in the future. Tell us.

Using your skills at writing memoir, you can now write it down and speak up. What we're looking for on the op-ed page are voices of authority, so you'll need to do some credible reporting to ascertain the facts and figures—how many patients worldwide, the status of current legislation, the senator holding up that legislation—after which your reader will know what to do by changing her vote, making that call, or sending that check.

The timing of op-eds is key and, like everything else in the newspaper, is dictated by what is known as the "news peg." This is the reason the piece appears on a particular day or in a certain season— it's Mother's Day, for instance, or stroke awareness month. News pegs are essential even to blog posts: We read about soup in winter (unless it's chilled soup, of course), shaping up for swim season in spring, and cooling down in summer. Knowing when to tell your tale is essential to your success, by assuring your reader that you are informed about what is going on in the world and are reacting from an informed place. Bloggers and Tweeters forget this all the time, thinking that just because it happened to them at this moment, I might be interested. They're wrong. But now you know to take notes and file them by season, planning your work around the calendar. Do so, and when there is breaking news that is on your topic, you can make your move. If you've been writing all along with the hope of one day publishing on your family's hereditary disease or its third-generation shrimping business, yours will be the voice we want to read when research gets slashed or the next oil rig pollutes our planet.

Using your personal tale to illustrate a larger topic is an unsung wonder of memoir. So read those op-ed pages, and rock the world.

KISSING VINNIE

One night while single and living in Manhattan, I met a beautiful young man named Vinnie. Considerably younger than I, he could have stepped in—or out of—any of the supporting roles in *Saturday Night Fever*. Still living at home with "Ma," he worked in construction and had spaghetti every Sunday night. We had only a few dates, the last of which ended during a good-night kiss, when he pulled away and asked, "Yo. Who's kissing who here?" A good phrase to remember when making that daunting transition from a vomit draft to a finished piece. Who's doing the kissing, you might ask, and who am I choosing to kiss?

Of all the people you are, who are you in the piece? Will you write from the first-person point of view, the "I"? Will you write from the second person, speaking directly to the reader? Will you use the third person and hover in an omniscient voice, reporting on something from the outside rather than from the personal point of view? And what's your expertise? Are you a beginning baker writing a food blog about learning to bake? That will be your point of view, your personality, and it will be reflected in how you approach your topics. An expert baker has a wholly different set of goals and therefore a different tone, one that commands, while the newbie can be charmingly naïve, though both narrators may be passionately committed to the art of baking.

Who are you making out with? Where will this piece appear? On your blog? No one knows better than you what defines your blog, so you're good. A personal essay for the *New York Times Magazine*? Have you read it religiously for a good, long time? You must, you know.

In my class I always ask, "Who wants to write for the *New Yorker*?" And everyone's hands shoot up. Then I ask, "Who reads the *New Yorker*?" and pretty much no hands go up. You do know that while the *New Yorker* loves cat cartoons, they do not take cute cat stories, right? But other places do accept stories about you and how your cat changed your life, including *Cat Fancy* magazine and many cat blogs, and it's your job to target the right venue for your work so you can write to length and to the tone of the publication.

WRITING IN REAL TIME

Let's pretend you had a total breakdown this past Saturday at Chuck E. Cheese. Just saying. I mean, perfectly sane people do. And maybe you wrote it down in your inexpensive little spiral notebook on the way home, and you've pretty much got the whole scene scribbled, complete with the part where you feel quite proud of yourself for not showing your small child just how horribly shaken you were by the senseless tumult of the place. That's interesting. Not breaking down in front of children sounds like a marker on the way to emotional maturity, the kind everyone should have in place before being allowed to parent anyone.

So now you've got three things in the piece—a scene, some arrows that suggest a transition from a mere experience of horror to one of understanding something, and one good universal milestone.

My breakdown came just after my husband and I agreed to take our daughter and Ava, her best friend, to Chuck's. I told Ava's mother we'd never been before, that we'd be happy to do it. How bad could it be? She smiled a knowing smile. She may have patted my hand.

It all started as we opened the door and I was knocked back by panic. Reflexively checking the occupancy sign at the front door—410—I took a quick scan. We were surely beyond illegal. My husband checked my face for signs that I might bolt. Initially strengthened by his sensitivity, I locked my hand into his, looked straight ahead, and elbowed my way in. Ninety minutes later, we emerged utterly changed, and not just by the pizza in our hair or the ranch dressing that somehow got ladled into my purse.

Technically, I really didn't have the breakdown in Chuck's: I waited until we got into the car. What would have been the point in shrieking, rending my clothes, and throwing my food while still inside? I mean, there were already people doing that.

No, not until we were safe in our seat belts did I realize I was shaking. The quickened pulse in the vein of my neck confirmed my status. Slowly I turned to the backseat, not choosing my words one bit carefully, and said, "Well, that was—" and got cut off by the sounds of the two little girls swapping prizes, laughing about the games they had won, and vowing to return soon. They'd had a really good time.

Worried that I was alone in my dismay, I checked the side of my husband's face. He had visibly aged that afternoon. Good, I thought, we agree.

What I had liked about the day was the hour leading up to the din, when we had visited a planetarium, viewing a kids' guide to the stars and riding a low-tech space-shuttle simulator. The kids seemed to like that, too, but they loved Chuck E. Cheese. Chuck himself must know why, because those little girls couldn't wait to go back.

Later in the day, as I wrote down those details, knowing there was something to use here, I felt the pull of something slightly larger. On its own, it's merely a slightly amusing tale. But there's that moment there when the kids are happy and I am not. That's interesting.

So maybe I'll restart the piece by saying something like:

No doubt about it: Good parenting requires a healthy respect for forgetfulness and a working knowledge of when to use it. Women who give birth claim that after delivery they forget all about the pain. Since our daughter was adopted, what I've forgotten is all the preadoption paperwork.

That, and what exactly we used to do on Saturday afternoons before our daughter came along.

Did we sleep? Read? Eat? My memory has been wiped clean. And it wouldn't be healthy to stack up those long-gone weekend afternoons against what we do these days. There's simply no comparison.

Last Saturday, for instance, I had a breakdown at Chuck E. Cheese.

And then leave the rest of the piece as it was. Hmmm, but now I need that kicker.

So maybe after that line about how the girls cannot wait to go back, I'll circle back to my opening thought, using the bagel, and put on the end something like:

I was reminded of the value in choosing what to remember.

As we were driving home, a memory popped up, of Kiddie City on Northern Boulevard in Queens—long gone, but not forgotten by me, apparently—and of the Lollipop Farm in Westbury, Long Island, leveled years ago and replaced by a strip mall. I was about to tell my husband that when I was a kid, everyone always had a wonderful time at those places, but then I realized that it probably wasn't true. My parents probably shook in the front seat as my sister and I replayed each magic moment in the back. But I don't remember them ever mentioning it.

On Sunday night, my daughter and I reviewed the weekend events: There was that new movie we rented Friday night; the outing to Chuck's with Ava; her favorite babysitter on Saturday night; church; a brunch; and riding bikes together on Sunday. What did she remember as the best time?

She thought for a moment. "Being with you and Daddy." What I hope to always remember is how that made me feel.

Saccharine? A little. But who am I in this piece? Not my cynical self, but someone who is having that cynicism shaved down a bit by the simple logic of children. Can you one day be drop-to-your-knees reverent about your child and other days just want to hand the baby to the mailman while you mix a martini? Then you're a normal parent, one whose authority I would find believable. A reliable narrator, you'd have the voice I'd want to read.

And who is my audience? Where am I sending it? In my case, it was the *New York Daily News*, where I published freelance parenting columns, so the references to the long-gone amusement parks in Queens made sense. If it's a parenting magazine, remember that some are snarkier than others. Same with mommy blogs, since some are marvelously sarcastic and others are frighteningly sincere.

What's your mothering point of view? Sometimes that voice is best without aging—no time to think about who you'd like to sound like.

Writing in real time, you may scrawl down how you really sound and what you really felt, and we'll feel it, too, and it won't be some gauzy thing written to sound like today's hippest blogger. You'll sound like you, and that is a very good place to write from.

SELF-CONGRATULATIONS ARE NEVER IN THE MAIL

Let's say you've embarked on a piece that you think will interest women. The topic: how you've never been romantically swindled. No man has ever taken advantage of you in any way. It's a claim you like to make, are comfortable making, and think others should know about.

Well, that's not enough to make it a piece. First off, self-congratulatory is very bad. Think about it. Who would really choose to listen to another monologue from the "And then I saids," those bores who quote their own supposed retorts to a battered series of people they dominate every day? The "And then I saids" should have to wear buttons so I can bolt for the canapés as they make their way toward me in a cocktail party. We learn nothing in these encounters, after all, so why listen?

Can you edit that piece on never being had by a cad and make it interesting to others? Maybe. Consider the topic of teaching your teenage niece to be gigolo-proof. Now, that might work, since wanting to have some role in raising a sibling's child is the very business of aunts and uncles, and as you retool the topic, the voice will change. Your original version would have been smarmy, and if self-congratulatory is bad, smarmy is dead-skunk dreadful. Being the only one who's right is the tough sell it should be. And as you search through that smarmy vomit draft, you must start feeling your way toward a voice of authority that is more meritocracy than fascist state. That, coupled with your status as an aunt, will make us want to read you, listen to you, or perhaps even buy your book.

My father used to say that you should try to write everything as if it were a letter home, a suggestion that's both graceful and correct. In a letter home, you rarely tell those people who raised you how very great you are, or right you are, or unique. You tend to write about the ideas you are trying on or the things you've tried and failed; how scared you are or how lonely. You are the small dog when you write a letter home, telling them how you've changed or what you've witnessed, and while you might wish they were here, they're not. So get your facts right and put the bold, brash bragging aside, because these guys knew you when, and they can still kick your emotional ass if you get out of line.

So can readers, though they do so by not buying your books, not listening all the way through to your radio piece, and never again clicking on your blog.

GETTING FEEDBACK ALONG THE WAY

While pretending you are writing a letter home is a good way to go, any actual employment of your family at this point is nothing but trouble and may be as perilous as that vicious classroom feedback described earlier. Just as nastiness lays no pipe toward rewrite, überkindness also kills excellent writing. That kind of gratuitous support begins at home, where reading your work to someone who depends on you for food, shelter, or sex can garner only one response: "Nice," or worst of all, "Neat!"

You get a "nice" or a "neat," and you're toast. Either throw the piece away or go to a class where—along with negative gratuitous commentary—the words "nice" and "neat" are also banned. And while I don't know them personally, I do know that your homepeople just don't have the qualifications to do this work, nor do they want them. Their kind countenance will only string you along.

But "nice" and "neat" from someone who loves you is at least encouraging. You might get the dreaded "I don't get it" from someone who stood up and promised before God, friends, and the state of New York to honor you until the end of time.

Now what are you going to do? *Explain* the piece to them? It's like begging someone to love you. It has never worked.

You need someone who is invested in your success. This can be found in a good writing group or class, where you might also meet someone whose hard work and strong critiquing skills fit your needs—and yours, hers—meaning you can work together forever. Many of my students have continued on in pairs for years. Make no mistake, however: It's a big job, requiring far more than offering up positive gratuitous comments. When someone gives me his work to read, he has no idea how much work is required on both our parts.

While I want to make that thing sing, that's a minor issue. The real question is if the writer wants it to succeed: If I suggest the edits, will he go ahead and do the work?

I once knew a fine college president who, like all college presidents, was besieged with manuscripts from alums who think that college presidents wait by the mailbox for every graduate's next book. A well-bred gentlemen, he had a standard handwritten response on good stationery. The salutation: "Thank you for your recent manuscript. I will lose no time in reading it."

I've always wondered how many of them got the joke.

If you're willing to do the work it takes—the rewrites, editing, more rewrites, more editing—then you'll likely succeed, and no one will consider it a waste of time to read your stuff.

Already dead, page 86

The most-asked question in my class is "How do I know when it's done?" In fact, a piece of writing never really dies, though you are done when a blog post, an essay, even a book has fulfilled the small task you assigned it. If you read your piece even minutes after publication, you'll see things you would have changed.

Your work is decidedly not done after a mere vomit draft and some rearrangement of that draft. In class, before reading a piece, the writer tells us what draft it is so we know what to look for to help her succeed, since as a piece gets closer to being finished, the editing should become more precise. For instance, while there is limited value in discussing the adjectives used in a vomit draft, in a later rewrite, it will be those very descriptors that can make or break the piece.

The *Times Magazine* editor who sat with me night after night went way beyond his job description, as did Nan Talese, my first book editor, who moved through my manuscript one word at a time over the eighteen months it took to write and rewrite it. Then the book went out to a freelance editor, and back it came to me with demands, directions, and declarations, one of which sent me to bed for days.

In my twenties, I quit my job at the *New York Times* to write that book, a move made against the advice of pretty much everyone I knew. I was feeling pretty damn saucy until that edit came back to me. There, in the margin of page 110, after an impassioned rendering of the death of my beloved father, the copyeditor had scrawled coolly, "Already dead, page 86."

Apparently, I was not done.

Chapter 5

Life in the Morgue

IN THE DAYS after September 11 while we scrambled for something to say, I couldn't think of anything to add to the dialogue of anguish. So I went after the language of healing, remembering that in 1973, when my father retired after fifty years as a sportswriter in the newspaper business, he stayed home for one day and then took a job on the 101st floor of the new Two World Trade Center.

He loved the place, particularly the sway of the buildings, which, he explained, you really only saw lying flat on the floor with one eye closed. He assumed this position many times, and he could convince almost anyone to lie down and have a look as well. I was in college at the time, and he wrote to me at least once a week from his office, always marveling at the view with the whole joy of a man whose parents had raised him out of the tenements of New York and who was now looking out over a city he had loved as much as he loved baseball.

In his new job as the public information officer of the New York State Racing and Wagering Board, he answered questions mostly about Thoroughbred horse racing, the sport of kings. Of course, there are other kinds of fans of other kinds of racing, and when they wrote, he did his best to answer them as well. One day in 1974, when a little girl from Devonia Avenue in Mount Vernon, New York, wrote with a pressing request, he complied.

Dear Nancy:

I am told you that you are seeking turtle racing rules. I learn from our Turtle-Racing Division that the basic rules, under Chapter 4735.9B, Division X, include the following:

No cerise, polka dot, or striped turtles are permitted to compete.

The course is to be circular, at least three feet in diameter, with starts at the center and marshmallows on the outside—or finish—lines, for consumption only by turtles' owners and trainers and parents.

Entry blanks must be supplied at the course and must be filled in with full description, name, age, pedigree, trainer's name, and color (of turtle, not trainer).

Partnerships, stable names, authorized agents, and racing colors must be registered with the Turtle Club.

Stewards, designated by the Turtle Club, must be on duty to see that racing turtles keep to a straight course and do not go over the course at a speed that would be of hazard to other contestants or the spectators or stewards.

Any turtle adjudged guilty of excessive speed will be put back in his tank immediately and punished by being fed an extra amount of dinner. (The extra amount is intended to make him fat and thus handicap him in the next race.)

Any turtle who bites another contestant or a steward is to be frowned upon. The owner must practice frowning in front of a mirror for four (4) minutes before every race in order to be in proper condition.

No purse for any race is to exceed 4 cents, except in Anglo-American competition, in which the purse may be increased to a shilling, and several-turtle international racing, in which the purse may be increased to one subway token.

Talking turtles are barred, because of noisiness. No turtles may streak.

The letter was signed, "*Sincerely, James Roach, Director of Turtle Information.*"

I don't know what Nancy did with the letter when she got it, but I have kept a copy of it near my desk, and it has always reminded me of a happier time.

With that letter, and sparingly little else, an NPR essay was constructed and read on *All Things Considered* immediately after 9/11. Slender but hopeful, it was all I could think to do. Because even in the worst of times, spare is the ethic, the rule.

One of my jobs for two years at the *New York Times* was to write the weather "ear" for the front page, as well as the daily weather page, listing the exact highs and lows of the major cities of the world. Remarkably—or not—someone would call nearly every day to tell me that no, the high in Buenos Aires was not 57 degrees, but 58 on Wednesday, or that it had not rained the previous day in London, it had merely misted. People do love their weather.

Those calls were agonizing, but it was that weather ear that tortured me, coming on the heels of my former job as metropolitan desk clerk, with duties that included writing what's known as "refers," also for the front page. Weather ears and refers were never more than four lines, sixteen words total, one telling the weather and the other referring to news that would have been for page 1 on a slower news day but instead would be found inside. At the time, those sixteen words were the hardest assignment of my writing life. Nothing cute, not an extra word; it was the start of a life of learning that no single word, no matter how adorable, didn't deserve to die. This is an ethic you need to adopt.

MURDER, MY SWEET

In his prickly 1916 tome, *On the Art of Writing*, Sir Arthur Quiller-Couch (1863–1944) opines that you must "murder your darlings," and if there is a phrase more beloved by writers, I cannot think of it. People seem to adore it, almost as much as they rest assured that it applies to everyone's work but their own. Few writers are actually willing to follow this advice; perhaps none are memoirists.

When Quiller-Couch penned it, he was making the distinction between style and plain bad writing: "Style, for example, is not—can never be—extraneous Ornament." Later, he gave us his famous instruction: "Whenever you feel an impulse to perpetrate a piece of exceptionally fine writing, obey it—whole-heartedly—and delete it before sending your manuscript to press. *Murder your darlings.*"

Elmore Leonard later qualified this for a modern audience: "If I come across anything in my work that smacks of 'good writing,' I immediately strike it out."

When this topic is raised in my class, I default to a short talk on sin, and how from the first word you lay down, writing memoir will pretty much divide your time between committing sins of omission and sins of commission, during which you will soon realize that much as in life, what's left out may haunt you nearly as much as what gets included.

"But it's a lovely sentence," someone will whine, defending their darling when I edit it out. And that's the problem. It may be, but understanding that writing is not about those single flourishes, and instead is about the piece as a whole, is the first step toward learning how to commit the perfect murder—a good final edit.

TUCKING IN

The rest of the book is about editing. And while editing may seem to be the same spade work no matter what the topic or genre—typos, grammar, punctuation—it isn't.

It is savagely more difficult to cut scenes from your life than it is to excise a paragraph on school taxes or solid waste management from a newspaper column. We get touchy when told that the tale of the family dog has to go or that the funeral scene needs to be trimmed, perhaps by killing the reprinted twenty-seven-minute eulogy you gave. No one likes this kind of direction, especially when writing about a sick child or a deceased spouse, and as I suggest revisions in the class, some of my long-term students will appear to slide under the table, not wanting to make eye contact with either me or the person disagreeing with my cuts.

To make the piece work, it's essential to murder on demand. Family memories being what they are, however, they travel as a coagulated mass, clotting together around a theme—buying your child her first pair of school shoes, your first shoes, every single shoe you've ever bought. Those memoir pieces that don't collect data in a purely sentimental journey instead tend toward the academic, when someone less comfortable talking about emotions will link those little shoes to the family car driven to get those shoes, the price of gas at the time, the reason the child attends that good school, connecting all the way back to the Puritan rigor of childhood education. Either way, I've got murder on my mind.

If you think that editing out our kids is toughest, think again. The single topic that makes memoirists argue for every single sticky detail is the animals with whom we live. Prime territory for the treacly sentimental, pet pieces inevitably begin when a writer awakens at four in the morning with one great sentence about what dogs are in our lives, what dogs have always been, and what dogs are meant to be. I'm no exception. Having had more dogs than husbands or children, sisters or parents, I frequently make the mistake of thinking I understand the species, only to be utterly reeducated by a new and unique dog. And when an opportunity comes to write about them, I do, though each time differently.

How? By choosing a theme within the theme of the dogs in my life. This prevents the piece from getting too big or overly sagacious, and allows some repurposing of the same pets. Looking at dogs from different angles provides varying tales.

For example, I'm sure we can agree that *Marley and Me*, the bestselling dog book, is the simple story of the world's worst dog and what he did for a family. And when the author wanted to send out another sensation, he simply edited that book for kids, called it merely *Marley*, repurposing his topic and hitting a whole new market for another round of best-selling books.

When writing about our own animals (as well as our husbands, wives, and children) we'd be well advised to avoid any karmic-sounding sentences that make any grand conclusions. Keep it simple; let the reader make her own.

So when one of those grand-piano sentences awakens you in the middle of the night, maybe it's telling you what the piece is supposed to be *about*—that dogs change people in ways that people cannot change one another—and not meant to be shoved whole into the piece. Instead of using the line, show us what that idea looks like. Illustrate that ethic throughout the piece. We'll get it. And we'll buy it by the carton.

ACT UP, ACT OUT, BUT ACT

Watching an actor being interviewed, I time the talk, seeing how far in we are before someone mentions the writer who provided the screenplay and, by extension, the vehicle for the actor to appear on television in all that borrowed jewelry. It's a particular sport on Oscar night, and I can't help but notice how few people ever mention the text, so busy are they thanking their agents and Harry Winston.

Every so often, a celebrity interview pays big-time, as it did when the marvelous Mike Myers appeared on James Lipton's *Inside the Actors Studio* and mentioned an acting method called "heighten and add." Adoring him more than ever, I learned that "heighten and add" applies as well to editing. Explaining it, he then rephrased it as "Yes, and."

Heighten and add. Yes, *and*. Both work, both earning a place in the lives of writers struggling from the vomit to first to nineteenth—and finally publishable—draft.

Heighten and add. Yes, *and*. I'm going to needlepoint those words onto something.

ABE LINCOLN GIVES GOOD SPEECH

Which is not to say that you should make your piece longer. We are not heightening and adding, as in adding more words. We are adding to, as in adding to your message, upping your sense of fear, adjusting your timing, your syncopation, your joy. It's not volume we need. It's precision aimed at illustrating your unique point of view, and that's what editing is all about.

Need inspiration? Plaster Lincoln's Gettysburg Address to your wall, all 272 words of it. That's right. Two hundred seventy-two words, where, in its closing, he defies editing, defining for eternity the complex requirements of democracy as "that government of the people, by the people, for the people." Of, by, and for. Perfect. And then try to tell me you need more space to tell your tale. I'll tell you that you don't. And if you don't believe me, consider that Ann Coulter has typed up seven books and hasn't accurately defined "democracy" even once.

To successfully heighten and add, you have to be somewhat ruthless. It's hard when editing your own life. So I suggest going into the piece several times, each time with a single task in mind.

INDEXING

You have this argument, and you've told it using good writing math. So what does paragraph one add up to, and how does its math differ from that of paragraph two? What does paragraph two heighten, and what does it add to the foundation built by paragraph one? And charming little paragraph three, and four, and five, and on and on to the end of the blog post, essay, or book.

Paragraphs are furniture. They can be moved around. Looked at this way, they immediately lose their precious stature and become portable, even storable, for a more appropriate décor.

Print out your draft and write in the margin what each paragraph does. This is called indexing. "Introduces Louis" is a good index next to paragraph one; "height and weight" might be next to paragraph two (which you now know you'll kill if that's all it does). Moving on through the piece, you'll see if the points of the argument are laid out and if the math adds up to your conclusion.

Have you repeated yourself? Have you established the same fact, though phrased it differently? If so, that paragraph gets a "zero," and you must take sentences from each and slide them together.

And how about those paragraphs that go off in a totally different direction, bringing in an entirely new story? Hack 'em, though here's the message of the morgue: What you kill is there for another day, so put those excised sentences or paragraphs in a file where you can retrieve them later. For every piece I write, there is a short title (in journalism this is called a "slug"), so that in my computer this chapter will be in a file called "The Memoir Project," in a subfile called "five," referring to both the project and the order in which this chapter appears. Then for every semicoherent sentence or paragraph not on the topic at hand, there exists a new file called "five outs," referring to the chapter from which it was cut and suggesting a possible Frankensteinian afterlife, the tidy ethic of the morgue being never to leave anything lying around.

You, yourself, and you

After making the changes above, print the piece out again.

Starting again at paragraph one, search for all sentences beginning with "I" (and in any early memoir drafts, most sentences will begin with "I"). All those "I"s make readers as nervous as long paragraphs. They float off the page and wake that reader right out of the mesmerized state you're trying to conjure with your piece. We don't want that.

Circle every one and rewrite at least two-thirds of those sentences to begin with action. Instead of saying, "I ran over the good cat with whom I had come to live," edit it to read, "Backing the car out of the driveway..." and continue on, rewriting all the way through.

CERISE, CHERRY, OR MERELY RED?

Make those changes and print it out again.

Next: Adjectives and their nouns. Circle every pair. Are they up to the task? I can spend all morning looking for another word for blue. You can, too, and you're welcome into my world anytime, since it's at least as worthy a job as exploring someone's brain stem.

Don't think this counts? Consider "botched" in front of the word "abortion," or the fact that beauty salons never advertise "mustache wax," instead calling it "lip wax," and how we all stepped up to recycling when the "dump" became the "landfill."

I try to keep my French phrases to a minimum, too—to just one, in fact, the one I mentioned earlier from Gustave Flaubert, who knew a thing or two about writing. He wrote passionately on "*le mot juste,*" the right word. While it's worth reading Flaubert's take on this, Mark Twain does a good job of encapsulating Flaubert: "The difference between a word and the 'right' word is the difference between the lightning bug and the lightning."

THE WEAVERS OF WOODSTOCK

If you've ever visited Woodstock, New York, you know the place is populated by a distinct kind of person—artistic, flamboyantly individualistic. Perhaps per capita, there are more poets and potters there than anywhere else on earth. Many come to my class, and some years ago three young women from Woodstock taught me more than I taught them. All weavers, the group included two sisters and the sisters' best friend.

The first night, as I was asking what the class was going to write, the women—sitting in order of older sister, younger sister, and best friend—each replied that they were there to write the story of the recent death of the younger sister's husband: for one another, not for publication; it was how they chose to honor his life.

And I imagine that the world kept spinning and they kept talking while I wondered how I was ever so fortunate to be asked to assist in such a purely noble effort. For one another, not for publication, because it needed to exist. The very idea stayed in my head until the following week, when they came in, each with her version of the death.

But they had switched seats, the two women no longer cushioning the young widow. This time, she was last of the three, as first her sister read a piece about taking the call that no one wants to receive. Her sister was a widow. The best friend wrote of standing in the sun at the memorial, looking out over what would need to be the future for them all.

And then the little sister read. Maybe she was thirty, married for only a few years, deeply in love with her husband, and after I tell you the next detail, you will never forget it, perhaps even thinking of it most nights, as I do, all these years later, when I climb into bed with my husband. The night her husband died, her sister stayed on after everyone else left. At bedtime, she asked her little sister how he had held her at night, and gently cupping one hand on her shoulder and the other over her hip, just as he always had, they fell asleep.

That's the kind of detail you never edit out.

Two aspirins and a glass of water

Next edit: Search for unnecessarily long sentences. When you strive for short, simple sentences—the two aspirins and a glass of water of writing—those right words are the key, stating precisely what took whole phrases to communicate in your first rough draft.

Heightening and adding, all the way through. It gets better and better and better.

And shorter.

Boil, boil, boil

Each successive edit must be ruthless: Pencil in hand, touch each word in every sentence, make hard decisions. Is there a shorter way to say this? A cleaner, more precise way? Each phrase needs to be assessed and judged. Look at that last sentence. You could edit it down to say, "Assess each phrase." But that sounds dictatorial. Is that the tone you're after? Then do it. If not, if something slightly more friendly is intended, leave it.

You are editing as much for tone as you are for space, excavating down to the uniquely you, keeping in mind that yours is the voice we are listening to, and if that voice changes radically throughout the book, we'll notice, and we won't like it. Even though most good memoir is a story of some form of transcendence—I left; I sobered up; I got smart; I finally appreciated the husband I have—that voice must not sound like one sort of person one day and an entirely different individual the next. No matter what your chosen tone, we need you to be a reliable narrator. You need to tell us the truth and do it in a consistent voice. Even if you're doing the near impossible and writing from successive chronological points of view—one chapter from the perspective of your eight-your-old self, the next at ten, and so on—you must build that person in front of us, heightening and adding details that reliably add up to who you are now.

The goal of a good edit is for the piece to read like a sleigh ride: smooth and fast. It can, if not a word is extra, not a phrase is flabby. Here's the razor-sharp rule: If you find yourself skimming a sentence or paragraph, thinking the reader will enjoy herself later, forget it. That's not how readers work, and never how editors read. They don't say, "I bet this will get good soon, so I'll keep plowing." If editors and stay-at-home blog readers have one thing in common, it's that they bail out at the first sign of trouble, when the writing appears to be out of control.

And who can blame them? There is always something else to read.

The most basic rule of editing is that if you can't bear to read it, no one else can either. So when you find yourself skimming, commit murder.

GOING FOR PERFECT PITCH

Several times in this book, I refer to "the pitch," the way you sell yourself or someone else on your story, that precise bang-up, smack-down, slam-dunk sentence that makes the listener listen up and nod; one sentence that both encapsulates and delivers what your tale is about.

While editing, check back with that original pitch and see if you've done what you promised to do. What did you set out to illustrate? Have you fulfilled your obligations?

You may find that the pitch itself needs a hard edit. This is particularly true when submitting your work for publication, since that pitch will be included in any query letters to editors. Editing the pitch will help edit the piece, and vice versa, and while I've heard a bazillion pitches over the years, the one I keep always in mind when I write and edit is simply "I left."

Perhaps you left a way of thinking, a husband, or a habit. Perhaps you left one house and moved into another, and in doing so upped the ante on anything from your decorating to the drama in your life. Writing my first book about "the dramatic story of a family's struggle with Alzheimer's disease," I realized that to thrive—not merely survive—through my mother's illness, I had to let her go. Maybe you left behind a mere hairdo or an entire religious dogma. In any transcendent experience, we leave one thing for another, even if the forward motion can be measured in emotional millimeters. Realizing this now will help your editing immensely, since to illustrate "I left," the resulting work—no matter what its length—does not have to begin at your birth or extend to the last day of your life. Instead, the piece could be wildly successful by simply opening at the moment you decided to go and ending as you set foot on the threshold. We are fascinated by how people change and need little more than the moment of intuition to the moment of exit to keep our interest.

"I left."

Paste it to your wall and refer to it as you edit.

Reading aloud

At first, a lot of paper is used in the editing process: printing out a draft, circling things, editing them down. Soon you'll combine tasks, circling the adjectives and "I"s in the same draft, or catching them on the screen, editing as you go, saving all those trees.

To get there quickly, read aloud. Reading someone's copy while the writer reads it aloud—the method we use in the class—has made every single student a better reader. So at home, alone, I read the piece aloud to myself. At a very late draft, I'll read it aloud to my husband, whose tolerance for what he refers to as "purple prose" is excruciatingly low and whose ear is superb. You can try this now with your home-people, that friend you made in class, or merely read aloud to yourself, and you will quickly develop a highly sensitized ear to go along with that eye you've now got for the better way to say anything.

———

And that's it, except to say that when pressed for such advice on writing long-form memoir, the single best tip I know is to write five pages a day. No more, no less. The great Graham Greene wrote 500 words a day, sometimes stopping in the middle of a phrase, and at that pace sometimes wrote a novel a year. When I'm writing a book, I write five pages a day, five days a week, no exceptions. Start today, and in three months you'll have a first draft.

I promise.

All this, and T-shirts, too

At the end of my class I give out T-shirts that say "Write on."

Hokey, I know. Cheesy, but I don't care, since it's at least one rung up from the dreaded "Neat!"

And, anyway, I know you've been given far worse advice by other people.

So go ahead: Write on.

———

All projects have a punch list, including memoir projects.
Here's yours.

- Toss out your writing prompts
- Pay attention
- Write with intent
- Write what you know
- Include transcendence
- Be hospitable
- Tell the truth
- Make every page drive one story forward
- Ask yourself, "What is this about?"
- Use the algorithm
- Go small
- Take notes
- Refer to reference books
- Focus your lens
- Think in propinquities
- Be counterphobic
- Read the news
- Make your argument
- Map out your structure
- Vomit up a draft
- Plant your arrows
- Choose your audience
- Edit with murder on your mind

Acknowledgments

Eight hundred students have passed through my class—or maybe it's five hundred students, many of them taking the class several times.

Thanks to The Arts Center of the Capital Region (www.artscenteronline.org) for challenging me to start the class all those years ago, and thanks to every single person who has showed up. Thanks to my husband, Rex Smith, for the love he offers daily, for the hook in the back of my collar, for making way for me to be out of the house every week, and for sitting up late with me and delighting in my wonder after every class I teach.

Thanks to the people who have forced me to figure out how to do this, particularly to my students Mike Welch, a fine writer whose courage, brilliance, and stamina inspire everyone, thanks to Amy Sternstein for the careful read and fine corrections, and Paul Ehmann, whose poetry career was destroyed along the way to his success as an essayist. I don't apologize for the latter.

Thanks to Juliette Gutmann, a writer of enormous power, for listing those odd aspects of the course that might make a good book, and to the weavers of Woodstock, whom we only met once, but who changed everything in terms of understanding that every single story has 360 degrees.

Immeasurable thanks go to Tom Prince for a first edit worth its weight in rubies, and to Kenneth B. Smith for all the design tips on our sister projects. Thank you to Deb Futter, who bravely brought this little book to Grand Central, and Kris Dahl, who put it in Deb's hands. As ever, I thank my daughter, Grace, for simply being herself, my model in all things.

This book is dedicated to my friend Richard Young, who, when I go on and on and on about things, frequently reels me in with his knowing phrase, "There's something in what you say." I hope there is something here, Richard, worthy of the dedication on this book.

All of those mentioned above have helped enormously, but there would be no book, no idea, no word on this page—or any of the preceding pages—without Margaret, my big sister, whose brilliance knows no equal.